Christ Our Life

God Is Good

Authors

Sisters of Notre Dame
Chardon, Ohio

Reviewers

Sister Mary Judith Bucco, S.N.D.

Sister Margaret Mary Friel, S.N.D.

Sister Mary Jean Hoelke, S.N.D.

Sister Mary Cordell Kopec, S.N.D.

Sister Mary Charlotte Manzo, S.N.D.

Sister Ann Mary McLaughlin, S.N.D.

Sister Mary Donnalee Resar, S.N.D.

Sister Katherine Mary Skrabec, S.N.D.

Sister Eileen Marie Skutt, S.N.D.

Sister Mary Jane Vovk, S.N.D.

LOYOLAPRESS.
A JESUIT MINISTRY
Chicago

Nihil Obstat
Reverend John G. Lodge, S.S.L., S.T.D.
Censor Deputatus
May 22, 2007

Imprimatur
Reverend John F. Canary, S.T.L., D.Min.
Vicar General, Archdiocese of Chicago
May 25, 2007

Christ Our Life
found to be in conformity

The Ad Hoc Committee to Oversee the Use of the Catechism, United States Conference of Catholic Bishops, has found the doctrinal content of this catechetical series, copyright 2009, to be in conformity with the *Catechism of the Catholic Church.*

The *Nihil Obstat* and *Imprimatur* are official declarations that a book is free of doctrinal and moral error. No implication is contained therein that those who have granted the *Nihil Obstat* and *Imprimatur* agree with the content, opinions, or statements expressed. Nor do they assume any legal responsibility associated with publication.

Acknowledgments

Excerpts from the *New American Bible* with Revised New Testament and Psalms Copyright © 1991, 1986, 1970 Confraternity of Christian Doctrine, Inc., Washington, DC. All rights reserved. No portion of the *New American Bible* may be reprinted without permission in writing from the copyright holder.

Excerpts from the English translation of *The Roman Missal* © 2010, International Commission on English in the Liturgy Corporation (ICEL); excerpts from the English translation of *A Book of Prayers* © 1982, ICEL; excerpts from the English translation of *Book of Blessings* © 1988, ICEL. All rights reserved.

Loyola Press has made every effort to locate the copyright holders for the cited works used in this publication and to make full acknowledgment for their use. In the case of any omissions, the publisher will be pleased to make suitable acknowledgments in future editions.

Cover art: Lori Lohstoeter
Cover design: Loyola Press and Think Design Group
Interior design: Think Design Group and Mia Basile, Loyola Press

ISBN 13: 978-0-8294-2404-1, ISBN 10: 0-8294-2404-0

© 2009 Loyola Press and
Sisters of Notre Dame, Chardon, Ohio

All rights reserved. No part of this book may be reproduced, stored in a retrieval system, or transmitted in any form or by any means, electronic, mechanical, photocopying, recording, or otherwise, without the prior permission of the publisher.

For more information related to the English translation of the *Roman Missal, Third Edition,* see www.loyolapress.com/romanmissal.

Dedicated to St. Julie Billiart, foundress of the Sisters of Notre Dame, in gratitude for her inspiration and example

LOYOLAPRESS.
A JESUIT MINISTRY

3441 N. Ashland Avenue
Chicago, Illinois 60657
(800) 621-1008
www.loyolapress.com

13 14 15 16 Web 10 9 8 7 6

Contents

Especially for Families

A Note to Families begins on page v. There is A Letter Home at the beginning of each unit. A Family Feature, at the end of each unit, explores ways to nurture faith at home.

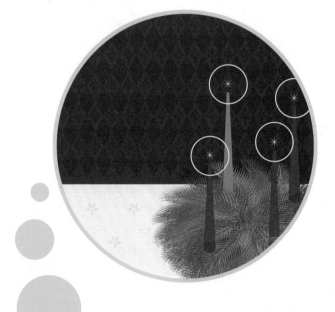

Note to Families

Goals of the Program

This program of the *Christ Our Life* series introduces your child to the goodness of God as a loving Father who has given us the gift of his own life through Baptism. Your child comes to know and love Jesus as his or her trustworthy friend. The program leads the children to a joyful awareness that the Holy Spirit is present in the Church and within us, calling us to speak to God our Father and to praise him by living as his children. Each lesson leads your child to a prayerful relationship with God. A Scripture prayer booklet is provided to foster your child's prayer life.

Format Designed for a Family Program

Each unit in the book begins with a summary of the message that will be presented in class. Each chapter highlights one aspect of the Christian message proclaimed in the unit. Usually a chapter is presented in class each week.

Because your faith makes a profound impact on your child, the *Christ Our Life* series provides a Building Family Faith feature, which summarizes the message of the chapter. Most of the family activities suggested in Building Family Faith can be done informally at mealtimes. The activities of Building Family Faith are set up under four topics:

Reflect suggests a Scripture reference related to the topic of the chapter. The reading may be done by a parent, a guardian, or an older child in the family.

Discuss as a Family provides discussion topics to help you and your child apply the Scripture reading to daily life.

Pray sums up the message for the week in a short prayer that everyone can pray daily. This prayer might be written and posted on the refrigerator or a mirror. You may add it to mealtime prayers or other family prayers.

Do provides ideas for things to discuss at meals, games to play, and family activities related to the message of the chapter.

In addition, each unit ends with a Family Feature that suggests family customs and provides review activities.

Visit **www.christourlife.org/family** for more family resources.

Note to Families

Educating Your Child to Live in Christ Jesus

It is our hope that as a result of the cooperative efforts of parents, children, and catechists involved in this program, your child will be motivated to:

- recognize Jesus as his or her trustworthy friend and speak to him frequently each day

- respect himself or herself and every person as loved by God

- listen attentively to God's Word proclaimed in the Bible and through the people who share his love

- participate meaningfully in the Sunday Mass by attentively listening to the readings and the homily; joining in the hymns, responses, and acclamations; praying the Our Father; and making a spiritual communion

- desire to be kind, fair, and honest

- ask for forgiveness when he or she has offended another

- be willing to give and share with others

- begin to realize that we are responsible for our choices and our actions

- understand and pray reverently the Sign of the Cross, the Our Father, the Hail Mary, the Morning Offering, the Glory Be to the Father, and the prayer To the Guardian Angel

Ten Principles to Nurture Your Child's Faith

1. Listen with your heart as well as with your head.

2. Encourage wonder and curiosity in your child.

3. Coach your child in empathy early. It's a building block for morality.

4. Display religious artwork in your home. This will serve as a steady witness that faith is an important part of life.

5. Gently guide your child to a life of honesty.

6. Whenever appropriate, model for your child how to say "I'm sorry."

7. Eat meals together regularly as a family. It will be an anchor for your child in days to come.

8. Pray together in good times and bad. Worship regularly together as a family.

9. Be generous to those who need help. Make helping others an important focus of your life as a family.

10. See your child for the wonder that God made. Communicate your conviction that your child was created for a noble purpose—to serve God and others in this life and to be happy with God forever in the next.

God Is Our Good Father

We are led by the Spirit of God.

We are children of God.

adapted from Romans 8:14

A Letter Home

Dear Parents and Family,

Welcome! Your first grader is embarking on an important journey and your support is crucial. This program is designed to provide your child with a simple and true overview of the mysteries of our faith. As they learn about the goodness of God and the love of Jesus, the children are drawn to respond to God in friendship and prayer. Your involvement and support will nurture your child's tender faith. Here's what's ahead:

Unit 1 introduces Jesus, whose words and actions proclaim his Father's saving love.

In Chapter 1 the children learn the Sign of the Cross as an expression of our friendship with Jesus.

In the next three chapters, the children learn about the goodness of creation and their responsibility to care for it. They also learn what it means to be made in God's own image and likeness.

In Chapter 5 the children learn how God shares his life with us at Baptism. They learn what it means to belong to the family of the Church.

The last three chapters focus on prayer. The children learn the meaning of the Lord's Prayer and are encouraged to make it their own prayer.

Chapters 1–7 each end with a review of the chapter and a Building Family Faith handout, which your child will bring home. This handout gives you a quick review of what your child learned and offers practical ways to reinforce the lesson so that the whole family may benefit. At the end of the unit, the children will bring home a Family Feature handout to help nurture the family's faith at home.

Visit **www.christourlife.org/family** for more family resources.

CHAPTER 1

Jesus Is Our Friend

We love our friends.

We like to be with them.

God is good to give us friends.

How can we be good to them?

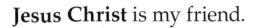

Jesus Christ is my friend.

He likes to be with me.

Jesus said,

"Let the children come to me."

Luke 18:16

Draw yourself near Jesus.

God is good to give us Jesus.

Jesus loves everyone.

We want to be like Jesus.

We want to love others.

Draw a picture of people you love.

I love you.

Jesus shows us how much he loves us.

A Moment with Jesus

Jesus is always with us. We can tell him anything. Talk to Jesus in the quiet of your heart.

Jesus died on the cross for us.

The cross reminds us of Jesus' love.

Jesus' friends make the Sign of the Cross.

We make the Sign of the Cross.

We show we are Jesus' friends.

We remember that Jesus loves us.

1

In the name of the Father,

2

and of the Son,

3

and of the Holy

4

Spirit.

5

Amen.

Color the hearts in order.

Red = Father   Yellow = Son

Green = Holy   **Blue** = Spirit

We Remember

Why did Jesus die on the cross?

Jesus died on the cross to show how much he loves us.

What is the Sign of the Cross?

The Sign of the Cross is a prayer. It shows our love for Jesus.

Words to Know

Christ   Jesus

We Respond

I love you, Jesus.

Building Family Faith

JESUS LOVES US with the love of a friend. He called his followers friends. He called the little children of Galilee his friends too. That means that everyone in our family is a friend of Jesus. He is always with us. He is generous to us. He wants the best for us. We can talk to him as we would talk to a good friend.

REFLECT

Jesus said, "Let the children come to me; do not prevent them, for the kingdom of God belongs to such as these."

Mark 10:14

DISCUSS AS A FAMILY

• Talk about the good things that God has given our family.

• Since Jesus is a friend of our family, what would you like to tell him?

PRAY

Make the Sign of the Cross—the sign that we are friends of Jesus and part of his family.

DO

Make the Sign of the Cross with your child at meals and at bedtime. Remind your child that this is a sign that shows we are Jesus' friends.

Visit **www.christourlife.org/family** for more family resources.

God Is Good

Our world is full of good and beautiful things.

God Is Good

God created the world.

He is the **Creator**.

Our world shows us that God is good.

The Bible tells us about **Creation**.

> In the beginning God created the heavens and the earth.
>
> adapted from Genesis 1:1

> God saw all he had made.
>
> It was very good.
>
> adapted from Genesis 1:31

Draw something God made.

The world belongs to everyone.

The beautiful things in it tell us that God is good.

God asks us to work together to keep the world beautiful.

What can you do?

A Moment with Jesus

Tell Jesus about your favorite thing in the world. Thank him for his goodness and love.

A Seed

One day a little boy planted a hard, brown seed in a pot of soil.

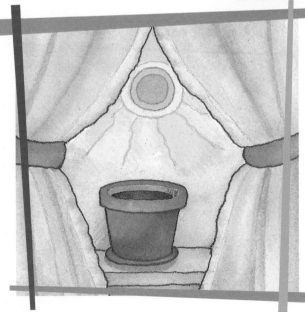

He put the pot on the windowsill.

Every day the boy watered the seed.

Every day the sun warmed the seed.

After a while the little plant inside the seed slowly pushed out a root.

Then the little plant burst through the brown soil.

The little boy saw tiny green leaves.

Every day he watered
the little plant.

Every day the sun warmed the
little plant.

It grew and grew.

Then one day the boy saw a bud
on the plant.

The bud slowly opened into a
beautiful flower.

The boy smiled a very big smile!

He was happy that he had cared
for the growing seed.

Draw pictures to complete the story of Creation.

In the beginning God created everything.
God created day and night.

God created the moon and the

sun.

God made every kind of

animal.

God created land and

water.

God made

people.

Everything God made was _____ .

good

Review

Draw pretty flowers growing in the flower pots.

We Remember

Who made all things?

God made all things.

Words to Know

Creation   **Creator**

We Respond

How good God is!

God is good.

Building Family Faith

YOUR CHILD IS learning that God created everything and that the world is full of wonderful and beautiful people and things that show God's goodness. God wants us to care for all creation so that we can help make the world a better place. We share this responsibility with God, who is present in our world and in the life of our family.

REFLECT
God looked at everything he had made, and he found it very good.

Genesis 1:31

DISCUSS AS A FAMILY
- Talk about ways that you see the goodness of God in our world: in nature, in the people we know, and in the things our family enjoys together.
- Talk about some of the ways our family takes care of God's people and the things he has made.

PRAY
"Give thanks to the LORD, for he is good, for his kindness endures forever."

1 Chronicles 16:34

DO
- Point out the things your child is caring for: possessions, a pet, schoolwork, and tasks at home. Talk about how he or she is caring for what God has made.
- At bedtime, make it a point to thank God for his creation.

Visit **www.christourlife.org/family** for more family resources.

God Is Our Father

God made me.

God made me like himself.

I can think, choose, and love.

I can smell and I can 👁 ,

and taste red 🍎 off my tree,

because I'm alive.

I can touch a fuzzy 🧤 ,

hear the purr of Boots my 🐱 ,

because I'm alive.

I can choose to 😁 or wink,

I can ❤ and I can 💡 ,

because I'm alive.

God made us.

He is our heavenly Father.

We are all God's children.

Draw a picture of yourself.

I am God's child.

God Cares for Us

One day Jesus was teaching the people.

He wanted them to know God cared for them.

Jesus told the people, "See how God cares for the birds. He makes sure they have food and a place to live."

Then Jesus said, "God cares for you more than the birds. He knows what you need. Trust in God."

adapted from Matthew 6:25–34

We Care for Others

When we share with others, we show we care.

Some people are sad, cold, or hungry.

What can we do to help?

A Moment with Jesus

Ask Jesus to take care of your worries. Thank him for his love and care.

A good parent loves.

A good parent cares.

A good parent forgives.

God our Father always loves and cares for us.

He always forgives us when we are sorry.

God is our good and loving Father.

VIP Activity

Write the names of Very Important Persons in your life.

V I P

V I P
You are a very important person.

LOVING: _____

CARING: _____

FORGIVING: _____

Draw a picture of yourself with your VIPs.

Trace the sentence in the clouds.

God is our good Father.

We Remember

Who is our Father in heaven?

God is our Father in heaven.

We Respond

I trust in God's love forever and ever.

adapted from Psalm 52:10

Building Family Faith

GOD HAS A particular kind of relationship with us—that of a loving parent. Jesus taught us to see God as our Father. Our Father in heaven cares for us, provides us with what we need, teaches us, and calls forth the best in us. Each of us—adults as well as children—can be secure in this loving relationship with God our Father.

REFLECT

"So do not worry and say, 'What are we to eat?' or 'What are we to drink?' or 'What are we to wear?'... Your heavenly Father knows that you need them all. But seek first the kingdom [of God] and his righteousness, and all these things will be given you besides."

Matthew 6:31–33

DISCUSS AS A FAMILY

Talk about the ways parents care for their children. These are hints of the great love that our Father has for us.

PRAY

Pray the Our Father.

DO

At the end of the day, talk about what God has given every member of the family that day. Say a prayer of thanksgiving.

Visit **www.christourlife.org/family** for more family resources.

God Our Father Is Holy

Moses was God's friend. He lived a long time ago.
He knew that God loved and took care of his people.

Moses talked with God. He listened to God.
He did what God asked.

Moses Knew God Is Holy

God spoke to Moses.

Moses bowed down and worshiped God.

He knew that God is holy.

Moses took off his shoes.

He knew that the ground was holy because God was there.

Moses showed that he knew God is holy. What did he do?

A Prayer of Moses

"Let me know your ways so that, in knowing you, I may continue to find favor with you. Let me see your glory!"

adapted from Exodus 33:13,18

A Moment with Jesus

Talk to Jesus in the quiet of your heart. Ask him to help you know the Father.

We Know God Is Holy

I am God's child.

I can kneel when I talk to God in prayer.

I can make the Sign of the Cross.

My actions can say to God,

"You are great and holy."

The church is a holy place.

Jesus is here in a special way.

We go to church to worship God.

Here are some holy things.

We see them in church.

They help us think of Jesus' love.

They help us pray to God.

Put a ✓ **by what you have seen in your church.**

We Remember God's House

Color the cross in the church window.

Draw some holy things in the window.

Fill in the blanks.

God is **HOLY.**

I am like God.

_____

I am _____ .

We pray to God in church.

Church is a

_____

_____ place.

We Remember

Who is God?

God is the all-holy One.

We Respond

Holy, holy, holy Lord,
God of power and might.

Building Family Faith

IN THIS CHAPTER, your child learned about the holiness of God. Everything about God is holy, including our churches. Church is a sacred space where we can experience joy, support, and strength in God's friendship. Jesus is present in church in a special way. Our family comes to church regularly with the larger family of Catholics to celebrate Mass.

REFLECT

But I can enter your house
  because of your great love.
I can worship in your holy temple
  because of my reverence for you, LORD.
Psalm 5:8

DISCUSS AS A FAMILY

• Why do we go to Mass? What have we experienced there?

• What else do we do at our parish?

PRAY

Pray the Glory Be to the Father: "Glory be to the Father, and to the Son, and to the Holy Spirit. As it was in the beginning, is now, and ever shall be, world without end. Amen."

DO

Talk about the holy objects in your home: a crucifix, a Bible, a rosary, and/or prayer books. Explain what they are for and their significance.

Visit **www.christourlife.org/family** for more family resources.

CHAPTER 5

God Shares His Life with Us

Water is a gift from God.

It is good.

Water gives life. It gives joy.

God is good to give us water.

We must take care of it.

You were baptized with water.

Baptism gave you God's life.

God is good to share his life with us.

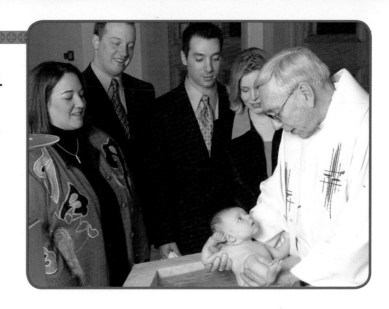

Now you belong to God's big family.
You belong to the **Church**. You are a **Christian**.

I baptize you
in the name of the
Father,
and of the Son,
and of the Holy Spirit.

At Baptism you received your name.

Write your name in pretty colors.

Alessandrobradocxa

Holy oil was put on your head.

Your parents, godparents,
and everyone else prayed for you.

You received a white robe and a candle.

They stand for God's life in us.

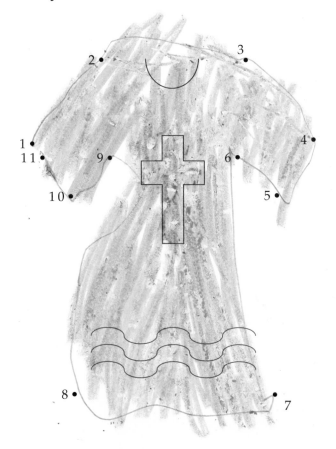

Connect the dots to see the robe and the candle.

Color the symbols on the robe and the candle.

We Live as God's Children

One day Jesus talked to the people about light.

He said,

"I am the light of the world. Whoever follows me will not walk in darkness, but will have the light of life."

John 8:12

Christians share Jesus' light.

They help spread Jesus' love.

Saint Julie Shares Jesus' Light

Saint Julie Billiart lived long ago in France.

She loved to smile. She liked to make people happy.

Julie became a sister.

She taught children that God is good.

A Moment with Jesus

Who is someone that needs Jesus' light? Talk with Jesus about how you can help.

Draw a picture that will make someone smile.

Write the facts about your Baptism.

Day _____ Year _____

Church _____

Name _____

I received God's life. I am a Christian.

We Remember

What did Baptism give you?

Baptism gave me God's life.

Words to Know

Baptism   **Christian**

Church

We Respond

Let your love be with me, Lord.

adapted from Psalm 33:22

Write m in each ◯, a in each ▢, and e in each △.

1. I sh▢r△◯y toys.

2. I h△lp oth△rs.

3. I s◯il△.

Building Family Faith

YOUR CHILD'S BAPTISM was a significant event in his or her life. Through Baptism we are marked as Christians, brought into the community of faith and born into the life of God. This is new life—a life in the Spirit. It is a direct participation in the love that the Father, Son, and Holy Spirit have for each other.

REFLECT

"In this way the love of God was revealed to us: God sent his only Son into the world so that we might have life through him."

1 John 4:9

DISCUSS AS A FAMILY

• How do we love each other in our family?
• How do we love other people—our friends, neighbors, and people at church?

PRAY

Lord Jesus, send your spirit of love to us. Show us how to love each other as you love us.

DO

Talk about your child's Baptism. Share pictures of it. At the next family gathering, ask family members who were there to talk to your child about that day.

Visit **www.christourlife.org/family** for more family resources.

God Speaks to Us

There are many ways to give someone a message.

We speak with words.

We use our hands.

We make a face.

How would you give these messages without speaking?

Come here.	It tastes good.
Good-bye.	I'm sad.
I'm tired.	

Draw a picture that says "I'm happy."

A Moment with Jesus

Talk to Jesus in the quiet of your heart.

God makes wonderful things
happen in silence.
Things move.

Things grow.

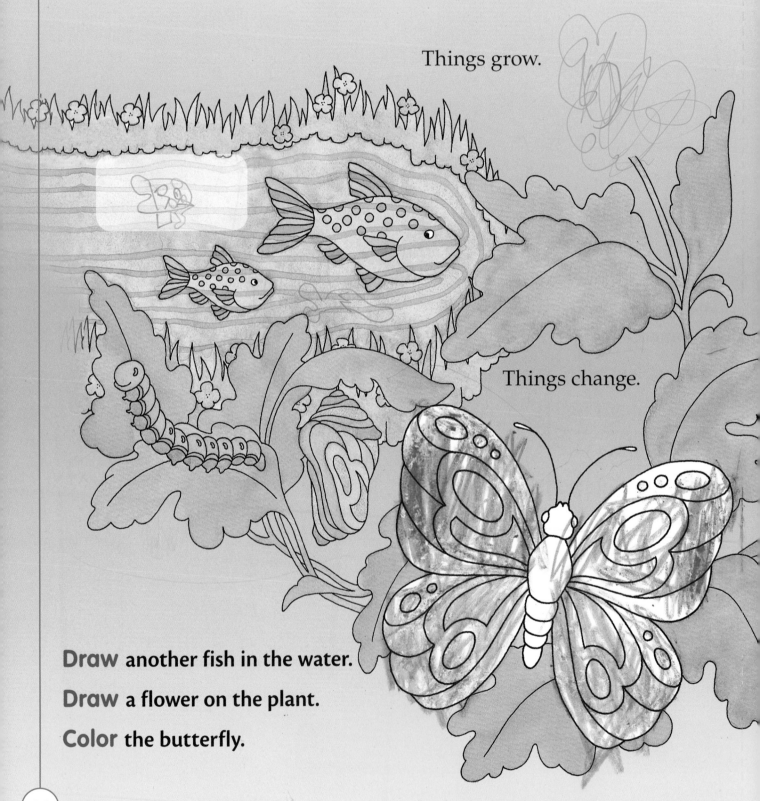

Things change.

Draw another fish in the water.
Draw a flower on the plant.
Color the butterfly.

We grow in silence.

We change.

Once we were little.

We grow.

Now we go to school.

We will grow up.

God speaks to us in many ways.

God speaks in silence.

Elijah was God's friend.

He liked to talk with God.

Elijah could not hear God in the wind,

in the earthquake,

or in the fire.

Elijah heard God in the gentle breeze.

God can speak to us in silence.

God can speak to us in
the quiet of our hearts.

God Speaks to Us in the Bible

The **Bible** is the Word of God.

The mother is reading a Bible story. The children are listening carefully to God's words.

When do you listen to God's words in the Bible?

God Speaks Through Those Who Love and Care for Us

God gives us people who care for us.

God loves us through them.

They tell us how to be good children of God.

God wants us to listen.

He wants us to try to do what they say.

Connect the dots to finish the Bible.

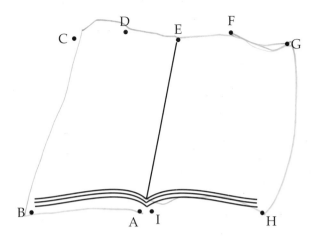

Draw a picture from a Bible story.

God's helpers bring us his love and care.

Who brings God's love and care to you?

_____

- - - - - - - - - - - - - - - - -

_____

We Remember

What is the Bible?
The Bible is the Word of God.

Who speaks to us in the Bible?
God speaks to us in the Bible.

Word to Know

Bible

We Respond

Your words, O God, are the joy of my heart.

adapted from Psalm 119:111

Building Family Faith

GOD IS NOT REMOTE. He is not silent. God speaks to us in many ways—through the Bible, in the teaching and worship of the Church, in the wonders of our world. God also speaks to children through the words and actions of those who care for them. All of us can learn to listen to the voice of God speaking in the silence of our hearts.

REFLECT
"Everyone who listens to these words of mine and acts on them will be like a wise man who built his house on rock."

Matthew 7:24

DISCUSS AS A FAMILY
- When have we heard God speaking to us?
- What do we say to God in reply?

PRAY
"Speak, LORD, for your servant is listening."

1 Samuel 3:9

DO
Show your child a Bible. Explain that this is an important way that God speaks to us. Read a few of your favorite verses to your child.

Visit **www.christourlife.org/family** for more family resources.

We Pray to God Our Father

Samuel belonged to God's people.

God spoke to him.

Samuel listened.

Samuel spoke to God in **prayer**.

God listened.

Samuel was praying.

God is my Father.

God talks to me. I listen.

I talk to God. He listens.

I am praying.

Speak, Lord. Your child is listening.

adapted from 1 Samuel 3:9

A Visit with God

A visit with God is like a visit with a friend.

There are many ways to visit with God.

Elijah visited with God in silence.

Samuel visited with God using words.

How do you visit with God?

A Moment with Jesus

Take some time to visit with God. Pray the words of Samuel. Listen quietly. Thank Jesus for your visit.

Elijah visits with God in silence

We talk to people we love.

They listen to us.

We talk to God, Our Father.

He listens to us.

We praise God.

How good God is!

adapted from Psalm 34:9

Write the words.

_____

— — — — — — — — — — —

_____

praise

We ask God for help.

O help me, Lord.

Come quickly and help me.

adapted from Psalm 40:14

_____

— — — — — — — — — — —

_____

asking

We say thank you to God.

I thank you, Lord, with all
my heart.

adapted from Psalm 9:2

thanks

We tell God that we are sorry.

Lord, I am sorry for having
done wrong.

adapted from Psalm 38:19

sorry

We talk to our heavenly Father every day.

We pray in the morning.

Lord, help me do what is right today.

We pray at meals.

Bless us, O Lord, and these your gifts.

We pray at night.

Lord, keep me safe while I sleep.

Choose one sentence below to complete.

Circle the sentence you choose.

Draw a picture to complete the sentence.

I praise God for   I ask for help with

I thank God for   I am sorry for

Circle a picture of something you could talk to God about.

We Remember

What is prayer?

Prayer is talking and listening to God.

What are four types of prayer?

Four types of prayer are praise, asking, thanks, and sorry prayers.

Word to Know

prayer

We Respond

I call you, God, and you answer me.

adapted from Psalm 17:6

Building Family Faith

YOUR CHILD is beginning to learn about prayer. Prayer times are times specially set aside for opening ourselves to God. We thank God for the gifts he has given us. We ask God for what we need. In prayer we can talk directly to God and share our deepest thoughts and desires with him.

REFLECT

"But when you pray, go to your inner room, close the door, and pray to your Father in secret. And your Father who sees in secret will repay you."

Matthew 6:6

DISCUSS AS A FAMILY

• What is your favorite time of day to pray?

• Share ideas about finding quiet times when we can talk to God.

PRAY

Your words, O God, bring joy to my heart.

DO

At mealtime prayer, thank God for the people who have shown their love toward you this day.

Visit **www.christourlife.org/family** for more family resources.

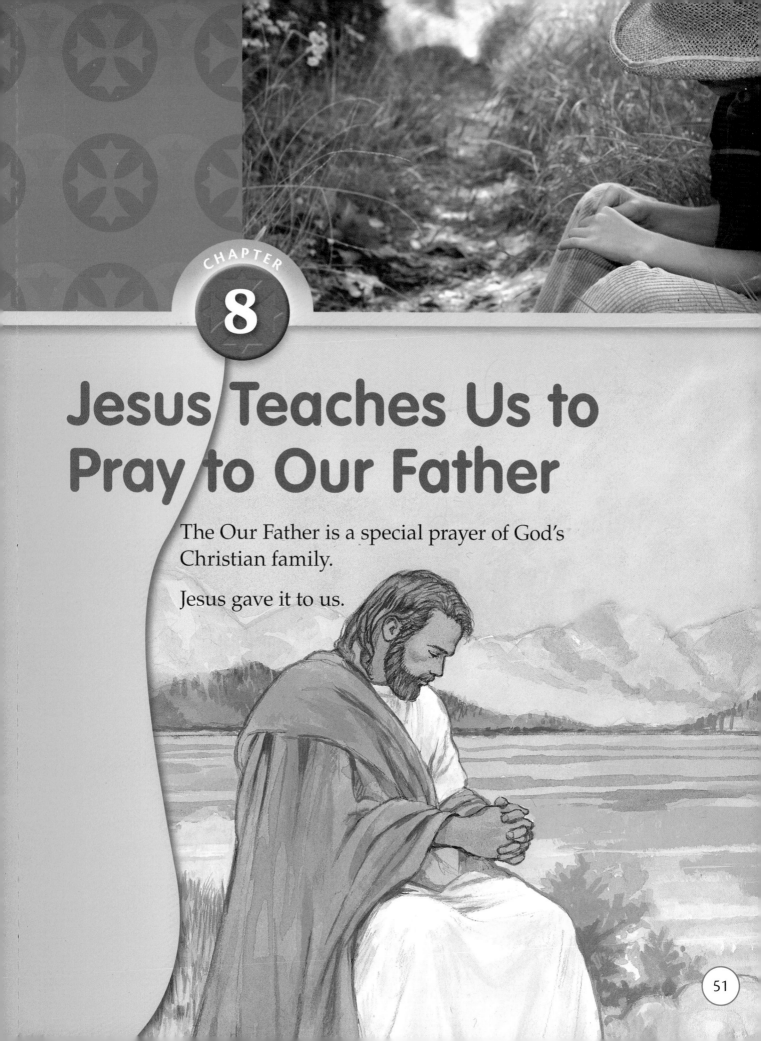

CHAPTER

8

Jesus Teaches Us to Pray to Our Father

The Our Father is a special prayer of God's Christian family.

Jesus gave it to us.

51

Jesus' friends saw him pray.

They said, "Teach us to pray."

Jesus taught them this prayer.

Our Father, who art in heaven,
hallowed be thy name;
thy kingdom come,
thy will be done
on earth as it is in heaven.
Give us this day our daily bread,
and forgive us our trespasses,
as we forgive those who trespass
   against us;
and lead us not into temptation,
but deliver us from evil.
Amen.

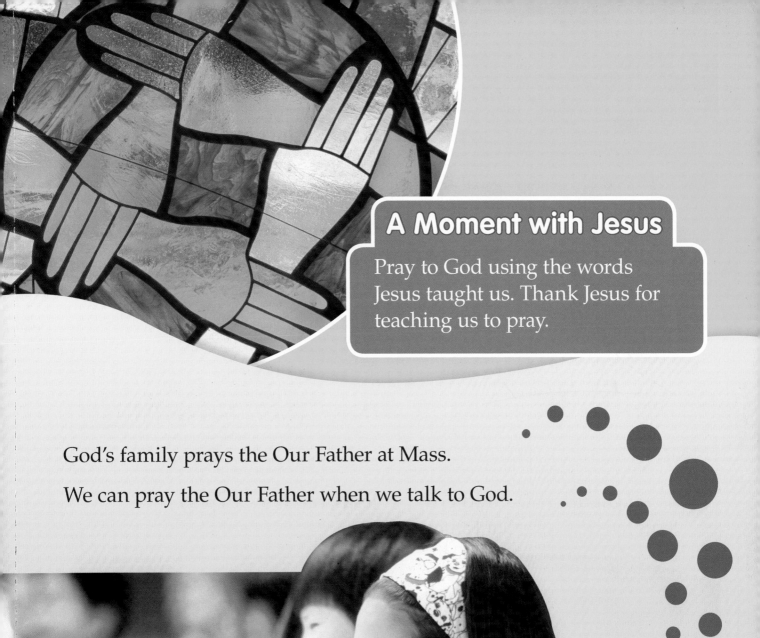

Pray to God using the words Jesus taught us. Thank Jesus for teaching us to pray.

God's family prays the Our Father at Mass.

We can pray the Our Father when we talk to God.

Circle seven words from the Our Father in the picture.

We Remember

Who taught us the Our Father?
Jesus taught us the Our Father.

We Respond

Jesus, teach me to pray.

Trace the path to Jesus.

What can you tell about the pictures you pass?

How would you respond?

1. Tara asks how to make the Sign of the Cross.

2. Luis sees trash on the school lawn.

3. Lydia says, "What is God like?"

4. Jeff wonders why it's good to go to church.

5. Kira asks, "How does God speak to us?"

6. Thomas wants to know how to pray.

We Love Our Good Father

Song   God is very good to us, good to us, good to us.

God is very good to us; God gives us all we have.

God is taking care of us, care of us, care of us.

God is taking care of us; we give God thanks today.

Reading   In the beginning God created the heavens and the earth.

God saw all he had made.

It was very good.

adapted from Genesis 1:1,31

Response 1   We thank you, God Our Father.

Song   For the gifts of your love,

For the gifts of your love,

O, we thank you, our Father,

For the gifts of your love.

We Celebrate

Reading   God made me. God made me like himself.

I can think, choose, and love.

Response 2   We praise you, God Our Father.

Response 3   I hear you, God Our Father.

Song   O we thank you so much,

O we thank you so much,

O we thank you, dear Father,

For your goodness to us.

Our Father...

Celebrating Your Child's Baptism

A child's Baptism is a very important event in the life of the child, the child's family, and the entire Church. It is a time for much joy and celebration, and it is something that should be remembered throughout the child's life just as a birthday or anniversary celebrates significant moments in our lives.

Celebrating the anniversary of your child's Baptism is an excellent way to help everyone understand how significant this event was. Baptism brought your child into the community of faith. It gave your child a new life—a life in the Spirit. It is something to get excited about!

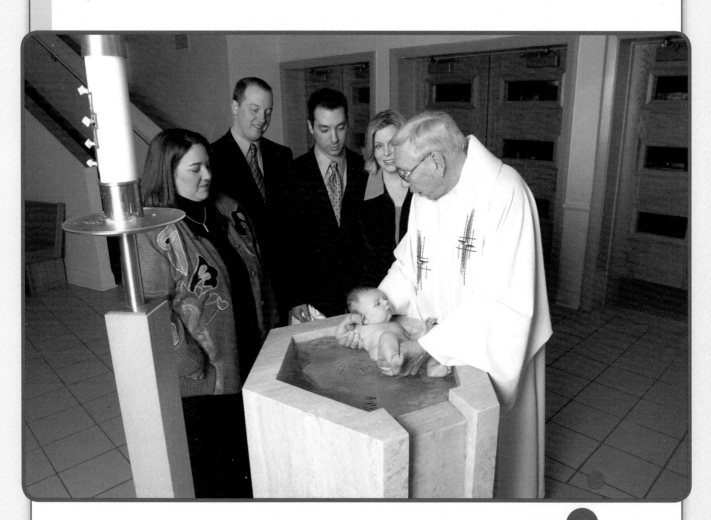

Family Feature

Symbols of Baptism

There are special symbols that are used in the sacred ritual of Baptism which you can use when planning a celebration of a baptismal anniversary. These symbols are used in the ritual to convey the momentous work that God does through this sacrament.

Water, the most important symbol, is a sign of cleansing. Baptism "washes away" our sins. Water is also essential for life. It symbolizes the new life of the risen Christ that is ours as Christians.

The **white garment** symbolizes the new life that the child lives after sins are washed away in the waters of Baptism. It is a sign of innocence and purity, and looks forward to the glory of the resurrection.

The **candle** symbolizes Christ—the Light of the World. The flame symbolizes the flame of faith which will burn throughout the Christian's life.

The **oil**, which the child receives twice in the ceremony, symbolizes our mission to live for others, and the strength and virtue we need to live this mission fruitfully. In ancient times, kings were anointed in front of the people as a sign of their service to the kingdom. Christians are anointed in Baptism as servants of the Kingdom of God.

The **Sign of the Cross** that is traced on the child's forehead honors God the Father, Son, and Holy Spirit, who brings the child into full membership in the family of faith.

The **dove**, often used in baptismal imagery, is a sign of the Holy Spirit. The Spirit comes to the child at Baptism, bringing the new life of God.

Preparations for Celebrating a Baptismal Anniversary

Make preparations for an event celebrating your child's Baptism. Involve your child in these preparations as much as possible.

What kind of event? You might plan a special dinner on the anniversary of your child's Baptism, a brunch after Mass on the Sunday closest to it, an open house on a weekend, or a combined birthday-Baptism celebration. Ask your child what he or she would like to do. This should be an event that you wouldn't mind repeating in years to come.

Who will come? Your child's godparents should be invited. If they live nearby, you may want to involve them in the preparations. Ideally, your child should have a strong relationship with his or her godparents. Try to include people from outside the family on your guest list. Baptism made your child part of a family of faith that extends far beyond blood relatives.

Plan the invitations. Have your child help with the invitations. Decorate them with baptismal symbols—a dove, a candle, a baptismal font, or flowing water. When the time comes, your child can sign them and send them. This should assure a good turnout!

Plan the food and decorations. Include some of your child's favorite things to eat. You might allow your child pick the main course or the dessert. Get started on decorations—a candle to light (preferably your child's baptismal candle) and placemats that include symbols of Baptism. Find pictures of your child's Baptism and have them handy.

Honor your child's spiritual development. Guests can be invited to say one thing they have noticed about your child that shows growth in faith. Examples: "I recognize how kind you were to the new student who joined your class this year," "I see how responsible you are in carrying out your duties taking care of your pet," or "You bring so much joy to the family through your positive outlook."

Pray. Plan a time of prayer. Use the prayer service on the next page, or adapt it to fit your celebration.

Invitation

What: Baptismal Anniversary

When: Sunday, October 8, 2006

Time: 1:00 – 3:00pm

Where: 123 Apple Drive

Mahwah, NJ

Matthew, Baptism

Family Feature

A Prayer Service for a Baptismal Anniversary

Materials needed: bowl with water, a Bible, and a candle
(the child's baptismal candle, if possible)

Select a leader and a reader. Open the Bible to Ephesians 4:1–6.
(Other good passages for Baptism are Romans 6:3–5 and Galatians 3: 26–28).

Set the bowl of water on a table. Place a lit candle near the bowl.
Gather around the table.

Leader: Today is the day that you, [*name*], were baptized. On this day you received new life in Christ and were welcomed into the Church. Today we will again sign you with the cross, to remember that you were baptized in the name of the Father, and of the Son, and of the Holy Spirit. Let us listen to the words of Scripture.

Reader: A reading from the Letter to the Ephesians.

I, then, a prisoner for the Lord, urge you to live in a manner worthy of the call you have received, with all humility and gentleness, with patience, bearing with one another through love, striving to preserve the unity of the spirit through the bond of peace: one body and one Spirit, as you were also called to the one hope of your call; one Lord, one faith, one baptism; one God and Father of all, who is over all and through all and in all.

Reader: The Word of the Lord.

All: Thanks be to God.

Leader: In Baptism we have been filled with the light of Christ. May we walk always as children of the light and keep the flame of faith alive in our hearts. May we live each day knowing our true identity as beloved children of God. And when the Lord comes, may we go out to meet him with all the saints in the heavenly kingdom to live with him forever and ever.

All: Amen.

Invite the group to make the Sign of the Cross on the child's forehead; then invite everyone to sign their own foreheads with holy water. Offer hugs all around.

Visit **www.christourlife.org/family** for more family resources.

God Sent His Son as Our Savior

God loved the world very much.
He gave his only Son.

adapted from John 3:16

A Letter Home

Dear Parents and Family,

In Unit 2 your first grader learns about God's great gift to us. He or she is presented with lessons on the goodness and mercy of God, who sent his Son to be our Savior. You can help your child take this message to heart by reviewing the chapters together and praying as a family.

In Chapter 9 the children are taught about Adam and Eve and God's desire that they live with him forever. They learn about the effects of sin and how God showed mercy by promising a Redeemer. The Redeemer is Jesus, the Son of God, who wins back for the human family a share in God's life here on earth and the possibility of eternal happiness in heaven.

Chapters 10 and 11 show how God kept his promise to send a Savior and prepare a special people to be his own. God chose Mary and Joseph to prepare for Jesus' coming. With Jesus' birth in Bethlehem, God became human like us (in all things except sin) and dwelled among us. These lessons prepare the children for a meaningful celebration of the seasons of Advent and Christmas. Talking with your child about these lessons can add wonder to your own experience of Advent and Christmas, too.

In the last chapter of Unit 2, the children are led to share God's love with everyone, especially with the members of their families. Please notice the times they do so and offer them encouraging words.

Chapters 9–11 each end with a review and a Building Family Faith handout, which your child will bring home. This handout gives you a quick review of what your child learned and offers practical ways to reinforce the lesson so that the whole family may benefit. At the end of the unit, the children will bring home a Family Feature handout to help nurture the family's faith at home.

Visit **www.christourlife.org/family** for more family resources.

CHAPTER

9

God Promised a Savior

The Bible tells the story of Creation.

Long ago God created the whole world.

First he made the sky.

Then he made the water and the land.

God made creatures that fly, swim, and walk.

Finally, God made people.

God made people just like himself.

We read about the first people on earth in the Bible.

God made Adam and Eve.

Adam and Eve were happy.

They were God's friends.

They lived in the Garden of Eden.

God was good to Adam and Eve.

He shared his life with them.

He gave them **grace**, the gift of his life.

They could be happy with God in **heaven.**

They would live forever.

Draw plants and animals to make the garden more beautiful.

But Adam and Eve did not obey God.

They chose to live without God's help.

God made them leave the beautiful garden.

Adam and Eve were sad.

God still loved Adam and Eve.

God said, "I will send a **Savior.**

He will help you be my friends again."

Then Adam and Eve were happy.

God Keeps His Promises

Adam and Eve waited and prayed for the Savior.

He did not come.

Their children and grandchildren waited and prayed for the Savior.

He still did not come.

The people hoped and prayed. They trusted in God's promises.

God made them his special people. The Bible calls them the Chosen People. The Savior would be born from them.

God told the people to get ready for the Savior.

Write the missing words.

God said to the _____ people,

Chosen

I will be your _____ ,

God

and you will be my _____ .

people

adapted from Leviticus 26:12

A Moment with Jesus

Talk to Jesus in the quiet of your heart. Thank him for being our Savior.

Draw yourself with Jesus.

CHAPTER 9

Review

Whom would God send?
Write the first letter of each picture in the box.

We Remember

What promise did God make to Adam and Eve?

God promised to send a Savior.

Words to Know

grace   heaven   Savior

We Respond

Save us, Lord God, please save us.

adapted from Psalm 40:14

Building Family Faith

THE STORY OF Adam and Eve shows us God's plan for his people. God created human beings to share his life and to live in peace and tranquility. Our disobedience disrupted God's plan. In order to restore it, God promised to send a redeemer. Jesus, his Son, came to earth to heal us from the effects of sin.

REFLECT
"[H]e was revealed to take away sins, and in him there is no sin."

1 John 3:5

DISCUSS AS A FAMILY
- Why do we sometimes feel unhappy?
- What can we do to bring happiness to the other people in our family?

PRAY
Come, Lord Jesus. Be here with us.

DO
Make preparations for Advent, a time of waiting for the coming of the Savior. Make an Advent wreath and locate Advent prayers.

Visit **www.christourlife.org/family** for more family resources.

God Chose Mary and Joseph

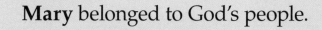

Mary belonged to God's people.

The **angel** Gabriel came to her.

He said, "Hail Mary, full of grace.

God has chosen you to be the mother of the Savior.

You will name him Jesus."

Mary said, "Yes, I will do what God wants."

Mary got ready for Jesus.

Jesus is God's Son.

Jesus is God.

Mary went to visit Elizabeth.

Mary went to help her relative.

Elizabeth was happy to see Mary.

She said to Mary, "Blessed are you among women."

Mary is the Mother of God.

Here is a prayer that you can learn.

Hail Mary, full of grace,
The Lord is with you.
Blessed are you among women,
and blessed is the fruit
of your womb, Jesus.
Holy Mary, Mother of God,
pray for us sinners,
now and at the hour of our death.
Amen.

Find the angel Gabriel's words to Mary in the prayer.

Find Elizabeth's words to Mary.

Joseph belonged to God's people.

He was a good man.

He did what was right.

God chose him to care for Jesus and Mary.

Joseph was the foster father of Jesus.

He loved Jesus and Mary.

Joseph was a carpenter.

He worked hard for his family.

We call Joseph "Saint Joseph" because he is in heaven.

Joseph wants to hear our prayers. We can ask him to help us do what is right.

God has chosen people to love and care for us. Who loves you?

Draw a picture of the people who love you.
How do you love them and thank them for their care?

A Moment with Jesus

Tell Jesus about your family.
Ask Jesus to bless them.

People love me.

Draw a line to the correct answer.

1. Told Mary she would be Jesus' mother

2. Jesus' foster father

3. Mother of God

4. Mary's Son, the Savior

We Remember

Who is the Mother of God?
   Mary is the Mother of God.

Words to Know

angel   **Joseph**   **Mary**

We Respond

Hail Mary, full of grace, the Lord is with you.

Building Family Faith

GOD KEPT HIS PROMISE to send a Savior. Jesus, God's Son, became man and lived among us. God chose Mary to be the mother of Jesus, and he chose Joseph to be Jesus' foster father. Both Mary and Joseph agreed to be part of God's plan. We too can do the work God has for us when we open our hearts to Christ's coming.

REFLECT
Mary said, "Behold, I am the handmaid of the Lord. May it be done to me according to your word."
Luke 1:38

DISCUSS AS A FAMILY
• Mary said yes to God. What opportunities do we have to say yes to God?
• What can we do as a family to celebrate Christ's coming at Christmas?

PRAY
Jesus, Mary, and Joseph, bless our family.

DO
Help your child learn the Hail Mary. Pray it every day as a family.

Visit **www.christourlife.org/family** for more family resources.

Jesus Our Savior Was Born in Bethlehem

Christmas is a special time.

It is a time to show love.

It is a time for the story of the first Christmas.

God gave us the first Christmas gift.

He gave us his Son Jesus to be our Savior.

God showed how much he loves us.

Mary and Joseph went
to Bethlehem.

This was God's plan.

Jesus was born in a stable.

Mary wrapped him in
warm clothes.

She put him in a manger.

Angels sang, "Glory to God in the highest."

A Moment with Jesus

Imagine you are with Mary and Joseph
in the stable. You kneel next to Jesus.
What do you say to him?

Draw yourself with baby Jesus.

An angel told the shepherds about Jesus.

The shepherds came to see Jesus.

Jesus, God's Son, came into our world.

This is the meaning of Christmas.

Color the stars.

Wise Men from the East saw a special star.

They followed it to where Jesus was.

The Wise Men gave Jesus gifts.

They told others the Good News.

Jesus is our Savior.

He came to save all people.

Draw a star in the sky.

UNIT 2 *God Sent His Son as Our Savior*

Christmas is Jesus' birthday.

Draw a gift you will give to him.

Complete each sentence with the correct word.

1. The _____

   told the shepherds about Jesus.

2. Only in a _____

   was there room for Mary and Joseph.

3. Jesus lay in a _____.

4. A _____ was over the

   place where Jesus lay.

5. The star led the _____.

manger

Wise Men

stable

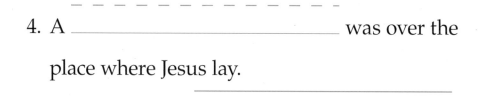
angel

star

Use the code to find the secret message.

A	D	E	G	I	J	M	N	O	S	U
1	2	3	4	5	6	7	8	9	10	11

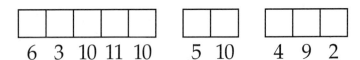

6   3   10   11   10   5   10   4   9   2

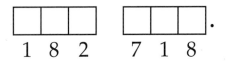

1   8   2   7   1   8 .

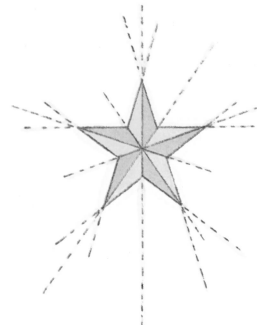

We Remember

What is Christmas Day?

Christmas Day is when Jesus our Savior was born.

Word to Know

Christmas

We Respond

Glory to God in the highest.

Building Family Faith

WHEN JESUS WAS BORN in Bethlehem, God brought about his plan to save the human race and heal us from the effects of sin. Jesus was a human being like us in all things except sin. That means that God experienced everything that we experience. The angels, the shepherds, and the Wise Men received the news of Jesus' birth with great joy. We, too, can be glad and joyful at Christmas.

REFLECT

"And suddenly there was a multitude of the heavenly host with the angel, praising God and saying:
"Glory to God in the highest
and on earth peace to those on whom his
    favor rests."

Luke 2:14

Visit **www.christourlife.org/family** for more family resources.

DISCUSS AS A FAMILY

• What makes us joyful? How do we react when we feel joy?

• Read the Christmas story together. What is your favorite part?

PRAY

Glory to you, O God. You are the savior of the world.

DO

Sing some Christmas carols together as a family—or sing them with friends and neighbors!

Families Share Life and Love

We belong to a family.

We do things together.

Each person in our family is special.

We need one another.

We love one another.

Jesus belonged to the **Holy Family.**

Each person was special.

They all loved one another.

Jesus' family did things together.

They worked and played together.

They prayed together.

The Holy Family was a happy family.

Write the names of the people in the Holy Family.

_____   _____   _____

_ _ _ _ _ _ _ _   _ _ _ _ _ _ _ _   _ _ _ _ _ _ _ _

_____   _____   _____

A **parish** is a special kind of family.

Priests, sisters, and many other people belong to a parish family.

Because we are baptized, we belong to the Church family.

The name of my parish is

_____

_ _

_____

People in our parish family care about one another.

We go to **Mass** to worship together.

We listen to God's words in the Bible.

We remember that Jesus died and rose for us.

Jesus offers himself to the Father for us.

The parish family likes to pray and sing together.

The parish family works together to help people.

They bring communion to people who cannot leave their homes.

They collect food for people who are hungry.

They visit people who are sick.

What can you do to help?

We Participate in Mass

We make a special sign.

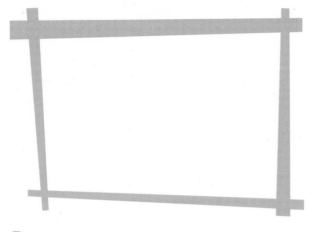

Draw a cross.

We sing songs together.

Color the musical note.

We listen to God's word.

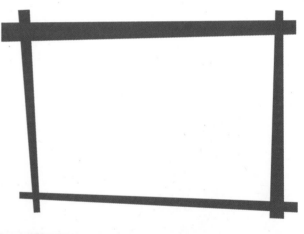

Draw the Bible.

We end our prayers by saying "Amen." Amen means "Yes. It is true."

Color the word.

Write the letter that comes just before the one in each box.

You will see a prayer.

H	P	E

C	M	F	T	T

V	T

We Remember

Why does God give us families?
God gives us families so that we can love and help one another.

Words to Know

Holy Family   Mass   parish

We Respond

How good it is to live together in love.

adapted from Psalm 133:1

Number the pictures in order.

We Thank the Father for His Son Jesus

Song God, God, thank you God.

Thank you for your Son.

He gives us hope, he gives us life.

Thank you for your Son.

Reading God loved the world very much.

He gave his only Son.

Everyone who believes in Jesus will not die.

They will have eternal life.

adapted from John 3:16

Response 1 We believe in you, Jesus.

Litany

We thank you for

- the archangel Gabriel.
- Mary the Mother of God.
- Mary's relative Elizabeth.
- Jesus' foster father Joseph.
- the angels who sang when Jesus was born.
- the shepherds who came to see Jesus.
- the Wise Men who followed a star.

Who else do you want to thank God for?

We Celebrate

Reading   Jesus is our Savior.

He came to save all people.

Response 2   We thank you, God our Father.

Song   Jesus loves me! This I know,

For the Bible tells me so.

Little ones to him belong;

They are weak, but he is strong.

Our Father…

Celebrating the Christmas Season

The Christmas season is a warm family time that is filled with powerful imagery and vivid customs that communicate the beauty and richness of our faith tradition. The season abounds in opportunities for parents to introduce key elements of faith to their children. Traditionally the Christmas season has focused on children, and rightly so. Christmas celebrates the arrival of the Christ Child, and it is a good time for your child to deepen his or her relationship with him.

Here are some ideas to help you make the most of the opportunities that the season gives us.

Explain the Christian Meaning of Christmas Symbols

Gift Giving

The custom of gift giving may be commercialized and overemphasized in our culture, but the core of the custom of giving gifts to family and friends is a celebration of Christ—the gift God gave to us at Christmas. The first people to honor Christ this way were the Magi, who gave the newborn king gifts at the end of their long journey to find him. (Matthew 2:10–11) This background will add meaning to the gifts your child receives and gives.

The Date

We celebrate Christmas a few days after the shortest day and the longest night of the year, December 21. By December 25, we can notice that days are growing longer, and the nights are shorter. Christ our Light has come, bringing spiritual light to a world tinged by spiritual darkness.

Holly and Mistletoe

According to ancient traditions that predate Christianity, holly and mistletoe were considered sacred plants because they remained green during wintertime. Christians happily adopted them as decorations for this sacred winter feast.

Family Feature

The Christmas Tree

The Germans revered the evergreen tree as a sign of life because it remained green in the bitterest cold. We bring evergreen trees into our homes at Christmas as a sign of new life in Christ. The ornaments on the tree represent the beauty and abundance of the gifts Christ brings us.

Santa Claus

The jolly, gift-giving Father Christmas is based on Saint Nicholas, a Catholic bishop in the fourth century who secretly gave gifts to poor people. His feast on December 6 is a special celebration in some European countries. Read about Saint Nicholas at **www.ChristOurLife.org.**

Christmas Stockings

The story is that Saint Nicholas left his gifts in stockings that some girls had hung by the fireplace to dry.

Christmas Caroling

The tradition of Christmas caroling recalls the announcement of Jesus' birth to the shepherds. When the angel of the Lord told the shepherds where to find the child, a choir of angels suddenly appeared and proclaimed in song, "Glory to God in the highest" (Luke 2:14).

Las Posadas

Posadas is a tradition that originated in Mexico. It is celebrated wherever Mexicans and their descendants live. At dusk, a procession of children, singing carols and carrying candles, walk door to door in their neighborhood to reenact Mary and Joseph's search for a place to stay in Bethlehem. They are turned away at a succession of houses. Finally, they arrive at a home where the "innkeeper" welcomes them with the greeting, "Enter, holy pilgrims." The children gather around the Nativity scene in the house for prayer. Then everyone has a party, which features the breaking of the piñata.

The traditional posadas (which means "inn" or "shelter") happens every evening for nine days, beginning on December 16 and ending with the piñata party on Christmas Eve. However, it is often celebrated just on Christmas Eve or on one evening during the nine days before Christmas.

Read the Christmas Story

In those days a decree went out from Caesar Augustus that the whole world should be enrolled. This was the first enrollment, when Quirinius was governor of Syria. So all went to be enrolled, each to his own town. And Joseph too went up from Galilee from the town of Nazareth to Judea, to the city of David that is called Bethlehem, because he was of the house and family of David, to be enrolled with Mary, his betrothed, who was with child.

While they were there, the time came for her to have her child, and she gave birth to her firstborn son. She wrapped him in swaddling clothes and laid him in a manger, because there was no room for them in the inn.

Now there were shepherds in that region living in the fields and keeping the night watch over their flock. The angel of the Lord appeared to them and the glory of the Lord shone around them, and they were struck with great fear. The angel said to them, "Do not be afraid; for behold, I proclaim to you good news of great joy that will be for all the people. For today in the city of David a savior has been born for you who is Messiah and Lord. And this will be a sign for you: you will find an infant wrapped in swaddling clothes and lying in a manger." And suddenly there was a multitude of the heavenly host with the angel, praising God and saying:

"Glory to God in the highest
and on earth peace to those on whom his
    favor rests."

When the angels went away from them to heaven, the shepherds said to one another, "Let us go, then, to Bethlehem to see this thing that has taken place, which the Lord has made known to us." So they went in haste and found Mary and Joseph, and the infant lying in the manger. When they saw this, they made known the message that had been told them about this child. All who heard it were amazed by what had been told them by the shepherds. Luke 2:1–18

Family Feature

Find the Story Behind Christmas Stories

Children hear, watch, and enjoy many Christmas stories this time of year. Help your child notice how the stories usually echo the themes and values of the Bible's account of how a great king, born in the humblest circumstances, exalts the lowly, confounds the powerful, and brings salvation.

How the Grinch Stole Christmas A nasty ogre terrorizes decent people, but a little child, Cindy Lou Who, sees good in him. Cindy Lou reaches out to the Grinch and he has a change of heart.

Rudolph the Red-Nosed Reindeer When strong, powerful reindeer run into serious trouble, a lowly reindeer saves the day. This completely unexpected turn of events bring great joy to the world.

A Charlie Brown Christmas Protesting the commercialization of Christmas, Charlie Brown buys a pathetic-looking but real Christmas tree instead of a glittering artificial tree. He is mocked for it, but Charlie and his friends learn the real meaning of Christmas when Linus tells the story of Jesus' birth from the Bible.

A Christmas Carol The Christmas spirit of joy and new life penetrates the hard heart of Ebenezer Scrooge, transforming the bitter miser into a generous and kind man.

The Little Drummer Boy A young boy of humble origin grows to distrust and hate people after his family is killed and he is betrayed by two showmen. His life begins to change when he meets three kings and follows them as they follow the Star of Bethlehem. Finally, when the boy encounters the Christ Child, he learns to how to let go of hatred and embrace the true spirit of Christmas.

Portray the First Christmas with a Nativity Scene

The Christmas crèche (French for "crib" or "manger"), which holds a place of honor in many homes at Christmas, was created by Saint Francis of Assisi. On Christmas Eve in the year 1223, Francis created a live manger scene in a cave near the town of Greccio. He used live animals and real people to depict the uncomfortable, humble setting of Jesus' birth. During midnight Mass at the cave, people reported seeing a baby miraculously appear in the manger. The practice spread rapidly, and soon the custom of a home crèche, with figures depicting the Holy Family, the Magi, and animals, became a cherished Christmas tradition.

Children are fascinated by the crèche figures. Many families place the figures in the crèche one by one during the weeks of Advent. On Christmas Eve the whole family gathers around the crèche, and the final figure—the baby Jesus—is placed in the crib. A child reads the Christmas story from chapter 2 of Luke. The ceremony ends with the family singing a Christmas hymn.

Visit **www.christourlife.org/family** for more family resources.

Jesus Shows Us He Is Good

The LORD is gracious and merciful,

    slow to anger and abounding in love.

The LORD is good to all,

    compassionate to every creature.

All your works give you thanks, O LORD

    and your faithful bless you.

Psalm 145:8–10

A Letter Home

Dear Parents and Family,

In Unit 3 your first grader comes to know Jesus the teacher. Jesus teaches in many ways—by what he says, by what he does, by the way he lived, and especially by who he is. Jesus teaches us to love God with all our hearts and to love others as he loves us.

Early in his public ministry Jesus chose 12 friends to be his first apostles. The children learn that they can be Jesus' helpers too.

The life of Jesus reveals so much about who God is and what God desires for us. Jesus is quick to heal people and show them God's care. He teaches us how to respond to that care with our whole hearts. He shows us how to pray.

Jesus tells the people that he is the Good Shepherd who came to seek out those who have strayed from the right path and to help them return to God. He teaches that forgiveness is always possible, and we learn it is good to seek forgiveness from one another and from God.

In a celebration of what they have learned, the children create new bonds of love and forgiveness between God, themselves, and others. You can keep that spirit alive at home by fostering a climate where forgiveness is freely offered and accepted.

Chapters 13–17 each end with a review and a Building Family Faith handout, which your child will bring home. This handout gives you a quick review of what your child learned and offers practical ways to reinforce the lesson so that the whole family may benefit. At the end of the unit, the children will bring home a Family Feature handout to help nurture the family's faith at home.

Visit **www.christourlife.org/family** for more family resources.

Jesus Calls Apostles

Jesus grew up.

He told people about his Father.

He called 12 **apostles** to help spread the good news of God's love.

Jesus wanted everyone to know how good and loving his Father is.

Finish the story. Use the words in the fish.

Jesus called ___Peter___ and
___Andrew___ .

He called ___James___ and
___John___ .

Today Jesus calls ___US___ to be apostles.

James

John

US

Andrew

Peter

Jesus calls all Christians to help build a better world.

He wants the whole world to be full of God's goodness.

All kinds of people help bring God's love and care to our world.

Families help children grow in God's love.

Priests, deacons, sisters, and brothers show God's love in a special way.

Leaders of nations work for peace.

Farmers grow food for God's big family.

Workers make things people need.

Artists make beautiful things.

Who else works to make our world better?

What can you do?

Jesus took care of his apostles.

He stopped a bad storm when they were afraid.

Jesus takes care of us today.

He is with us when we are afraid.

He may send someone to help us.

He may want us to ask someone for help.

Jesus helps us through other people.

To whom can you go for help?

Jesus needs helpers today.

We are all called to be Jesus' helpers.

Some people are special helpers of Jesus:

- Priests and deacons
- Lay ministers
- Religious sisters and brothers
- Missionaries.

Saint Frances Cabrini was a special helper of Jesus.

She wanted to be a missionary.

She wanted to tell people in faraway lands about God.

She crossed the ocean and came to the United States.

She formed a group of sisters.

They worked in schools and hospitals.

Draw a special helper of Jesus.

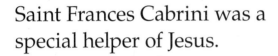

A Moment with Jesus

Say a prayer for Jesus' special helpers. Ask Jesus to help them in their work.

We Remember

Why did Jesus call the apostles?
Jesus called the apostles to help spread the good news of God's love.

What does Jesus call Christians to do?
Jesus calls Christians to bring all people to him and to help make the world a better place.

Word to Know

apostle

We Respond

May the whole earth be filled with God's love.

adapted from Psalm 72:19

Write the letter that comes before the given one.

I am a <u>Christian</u>
<u>D i s j t u j b o</u>
<u>helper</u>.
<u>i f m q f s</u>

Building Family Faith

JESUS CALLED 12 APOSTLES to help spread the gospel, and he called many other people to follow him and help him. Jesus continues to call people. He calls us too. Each of us, children as well as adults, can share in Jesus' work of bringing peace and joy to the world.

REFLECT
Jesus sent disciples to do his work with these words: "'The harvest is abundant but the laborers are few; so ask the master of the harvest to send out laborers for his harvest. Go on your way.'"
Luke 10:2

DISCUSS AS A FAMILY
• Discuss the times when you thought the Lord was calling you to do something.
• What work needs to be done to make our family, school, and neighborhood a better place?

PRAY
Thy kingdom come, thy will be done, on earth as it is in heaven.

DO
At bedtime, regularly pray for the needs of others. Ask God to show your family some work to do to bring God's love to others.

Visit **www.christourlife.org/family** for more family resources.

Jesus Shows God's Love

God made the world good, but some things in our world are not good.

People suffer and cry.

People are hungry and lonely.

People hurt others.

We all feel sadness and pain sometimes.

God our Father loves us.

His Son, Jesus, was a friend to people in need.

The Bible tells how Jesus showed God's love for people.

Jesus Cures a Sick Man

A man could not move at all.

Friends wanted to bring him to Jesus.

Jesus was teaching a crowd in a house.

The men made a hole in the roof.

They lowered their friend down on a mat.

Jesus forgave the man.

Then Jesus told the man to get up and walk.

The man stood up and walked.

Color the picture.

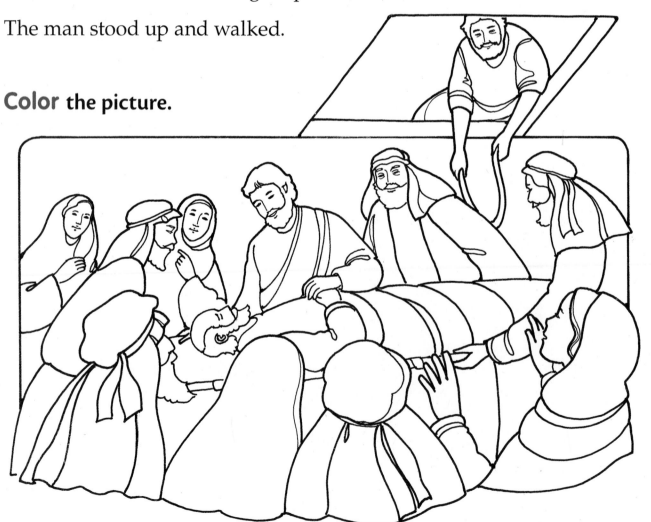

Jesus Brings a Girl Back to Life

One day Jesus was teaching about his Father in heaven.

An important man named Jairus came to him.

Jairus said, "Lord, please come to my house. My little daughter is dying."

Jesus went with Jairus.

But the child died before Jesus got there.

Everyone was sad.

Jesus went into the house.

He said, "Child, arise!"

The girl began breathing again.

She got up and moved around.

Jesus told the people to give her something to eat.

Everyone was amazed.

A Moment with Jesus

Think of people you know who are sick. Ask Jesus how you can show his love to them. Thank Jesus for his loving care.

Jesus shows love for people.

Match the sentences with the pictures.

Write the correct number in each circle.

1. Jesus healed sick people.
2. Jesus forgave people who had done wrong.
3. Jesus told people that God loved them.
4. Jesus gave food to hungry people.

Jesus brings God's love to people today.

Write the number of the picture that correctly completes each sentence.

Jesus heals when __3__ care for people.

Jesus feeds the hungry when we share __1__ .

Jesus tells of God's love when a __2__ tells about God.

Jesus helps people in need when we share __4__ .

Write e in each ◯, o in each ▢, and i in each △.

J◯sus l▢ved h△s fr△◯nds.

H◯ car◯d ab▢ut all p◯▢pl◯.

J◯sus △s th◯ S▢n ▢f G▢d.

We Remember

Who shows God's love for people?

Jesus shows God's love for people.

We Respond

Jesus, help me bring God's love to our world.

Building Family Faith

JESUS HELPED PEOPLE in need. He healed the sick, forgave sinners, and gave food to the hungry. He had a special love for people who were poor. Jesus calls us to do likewise because we are his followers. All Christians have many opportunities to do the same kind of good works that Jesus did.

REFLECT

"Come, you who are blessed by my Father. Inherit the kingdom prepared for you from the foundation of the world. For I was hungry and you gave me food, I was thirsty and you gave me drink, a stranger and you welcomed me, naked and you clothed me, ill and you cared for me, in prison and you visited me."

Matthew 25:34–36

DISCUSS AS A FAMILY

• If Jesus came to our neighborhood and our parish, where would he find people in need?

• What can we do to help these people?

PRAY

You listen, LORD, to the needs of the poor; you encourage them and hear their prayers.

Psalm 10:17

DO

Reach out to an elderly neighbor, a family member who is sick, or someone else who is in need.

Visit **www.christourlife.org/family** for more family resources.

Jesus Teaches Us to Love God

One day a man asked Jesus,

"What is the greatest law of God?"

Jesus said,

"Love God with all your heart."

adapted from Mark 12:28–30

Jesus loved God his Father.

Jesus talked to God.

He always did what his Father wanted.

How can we show we love God?

Write **the correct number under each picture.**

1. We can obey.   2. We can go to Mass.   3. We can pray.

Draw yourself doing something that shows you love God.

Write the prayer.

I love you, Lord.

At Mass we remember how Jesus offered himself to the Father.

We offer ourselves to God too.

We can pray the Morning Offering each day.

Write the missing words.

O Jesus, I offer you all I

think,   do,

Bless me and make me like you today.

Amen.

and say.

A Moment with Jesus

Pray the Morning Offering slowly.

The Apostle of Love

Saint John is called the apostle of love.

He loved Jesus very much.

He stayed with Jesus when he died on the cross.

Then he took care of Mary.

He taught people to love God and one another.

John's teachings are in the Bible.

Unscramble the word. Then write it on each line.

o e v l

Find out what Jesus said in John's Gospel.

Jesus said to his disciples,

_____

– – – – – – – – –

"As the Father loves me, so I also _____ you.

_____

– – – – – – – –

Remain in my _____."

John 15:9

We Love God with All Our Heart

Leader: God's love is very good. We celebrate good things. We celebrate God's love.

Song

Prayer Response

All: I love you, God my Father.

Reading

Reader: One day a man asked Jesus, "What is the greatest law of God?" Jesus said, "Love God with all your heart."

adapted from Mark 12:28–30

Reflection Response

All: Love the Lord with all your heart,
all you heart, all your heart.
Love the Lord with all your heart—
oh, give it all to him.

Leader: God loves us very much.
Tell God how much
you love him.

Song

We Remember

What is the greatest law?
The greatest law is
"Love God with all your heart."

Connect the lines.

I love God with all my heart.

We Respond

I love you, LORD.

Psalm 18:2

Building Family Faith

JESUS TAUGHT US to love God with all our heart. This means that we love him with everything we have; we don't hold anything back. It also means that everything we do can become a way to love God.

REFLECT

"Teacher, which commandment in the law is the greatest?" He said to him, "You shall love the Lord, your God, with all your heart, with all your soul, and with all your mind."

Matthew 22:36–37

DISCUSS AS A FAMILY

• How do the members of our family love God through the things we are already doing?

• What else can we do to show our love for God?

PRAY

I love you, Lord. Thank you for loving me.

DO

In this lesson, your child has been introduced to a simple morning offering. Pray it with your child before school.

Visit **www.christourlife.org/family** for more family resources.

Jesus Teaches Us to Love Others

Everyone Is Our Neighbor

Jesus told a story to explain God's second great law.

It is called the story of the Good Samaritan.

A man was hurt and needed help.

Two men passed by him.

Then a kind man stopped and helped him.

Jesus tells us to be like the kind man.

He tells us to love our neighbor.

Jesus told us that everyone is our neighbor.

We try to help everyone in need.

What do these people need?

Find the correct word in the word bank.
Write it on the line.

visit   food

friend   help

_____

_____

_____

_____

Draw yourself doing something that shows you love others.

I love others.

A Woman Gives All She Has

A woman who was poor went to the Temple.

She put two coins in the offering box.

Jesus saw her.

He praised her for giving what she had.

A Moment with Jesus

Thank Jesus for the kindness of the woman at the Temple. Ask for his help in giving as she did.

Two Coins Activity

Draw a problem.
Then draw how you can help.

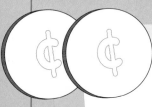

This is our neighborhood.

It is the entire world.

We are called to help people wherever they live.

Flip the letters below to answer the question.

What is another name for God's second great law?

_ _ _ _ _ _ _   _ _ _ _

golden rule

We Remember

What is the second great law of God?

The second great law is "You shall love your neighbor as yourself."

We Respond

Lord God, fill me with your love.

Building Family Faith

IN THIS LESSON, your child has heard two Gospel stories that teach us about helping others. The parable of the Good Samaritan teaches us that everyone is our neighbor—not just people we like or who are like us. The story of the poor widow in the Temple teaches us that God is pleased even when we have only a small amount to offer.

REFLECT
"Amen, I say to you, this poor widow put in more than all the other contributors to the treasury. For they have all contributed from their surplus wealth, but she, from her poverty, has contributed all she had, her whole livelihood."

Mark 12:43–44

DISCUSS AS A FAMILY
- Talk about people your child knows who are different in some way. What makes them different? Are these differences important?
- What are some small things we can offer to God?

PRAY
The LORD protects the stranger, sustains the orphan and the widow.
Psalm 146:9

DO
Help your child reach out to another child who is ignored or teased because he or she is perceived as different. Stress that even small acts of kindness and generosity are important.

Visit **www.christourlife.org/family** for more family resources.

Jesus Calls Himself the Good Shepherd

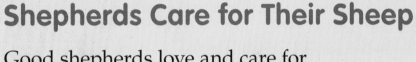

Shepherds Care for Their Sheep

Good shepherds love and care for their sheep.

They feed them and keep them safe.

Sheep know their shepherd.

They come when their shepherd calls them.

They listen to him.

They follow him.

Sometimes a sheep gets lost.

A good shepherd finds it and brings it back.

Jesus Is Our Good Shepherd

Jesus says,

"I am the good shepherd."

John 10:11

Jesus calls us.

We go to him when we pray.

We listen when he tells us to be loving.

We follow him by doing what he asks.

But sometimes we do not follow Jesus.

We do things we know are wrong.

We are like lost lambs.

Then we are sorry.

Jesus always forgives us.

He brings us back to his love.

Here is a prayer from the Bible.

David, a shepherd boy, probably wrote it.

The LORD is my shepherd.

There is nothing that I need.

He leads me to green grass and
    fresh waters.

He guides me on right paths.

I will not be afraid, for you are
    with me.

Your goodness and kindness
    will be with me every day
    of my life.

And I will live in your home
    forever.

adapted from Psalm 23

We Say We Are Sorry

Jesus is the Good Shepherd of God's family, the Church.

At Mass we say we are sorry that we have not always followed Jesus.

We say,

"Lord, have mercy."

We mean,

"Lord, forgive us and help us."

We give signs of peace and love to others.

We show we are happy that God has forgiven us.

We forgive one another.

A Moment with Jesus

Tell Jesus what is in your heart. Ask him for his love and peace.

Being a Good Shepherd

Pretend **that this little sheep is yours to care for.**

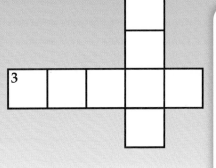

1. Give the sheep a name.

_____

_ _ _ _ _ _ _ _ _ _ _ _ _ _ _ _ _ _ _

_____

2. Circle the things that you use to care for your sheep.

3. Answer these questions.

Your sheep eats the flowers in your friend's garden. What do you do?

Your sheep is shivering from the cold. What do you do?

4. Use the clues below to do the puzzle. See what Jesus does as our Good Shepherd.

Word Bank

guides

loves

forgives

cares

Across:

1. Jesus ____ with his whole heart.
2. The Good Shepherd ____ his sheep.
3. Jesus ____ for us.

Down:

1. God ____ us when we are sorry.

Circle the sheep hidden in the picture.
Think about the ways Jesus looks for us.

We Remember

Who said, "I am the good shepherd"?

Jesus said,

"I am the good shepherd."

John 10:11

We Respond

**The LORD is my shepherd.
There is nothing that I need.**

adapted from Psalm 23:1

Building Family Faith

YOUR CHILD IS learning about forgiveness by studying Jesus' role as the Good Shepherd. A shepherd makes sure that the sheep do not wander away. If some do stray, he finds them and returns them to the flock. Likewise, Jesus is concerned about us when we do wrong. We can depend on him to forgive us when we sin and to restore our friendship with him.

REFLECT
The LORD is my shepherd;
    there is nothing I lack.
In green pastures you let me graze;
    to safe waters you lead me;
    you restore my strength.
You guide me along the right path
    for the sake of your name.
                            Psalm 23:1–3

DISCUSS AS A FAMILY
• How has God shown his special care for our family?
• Talk about how we often need help putting things right after we have done something wrong.

PRAY
Jesus, shepherd of our family, protect us from evil. Make us secure in your love.

DO
Pray Psalm 23 together. Use the version on page 117 of this book, or use the version in your Bible.

Visit **www.christourlife.org/family** for more family resources.

CHAPTER 18

We Come to Our Good Shepherd

God tells his big family to love him and one another.

It is not always easy to be kind.

It is not always easy to obey.

It is not always easy to do what God wants us to do.

It is not always easy to be a friend of Jesus.

Sometimes we hurt others.

We are sorry.

We can say we are sorry.

Sometimes others hurt us.

We forgive them.

Then we are good friends of Jesus.

Sometimes we come together as God's family, the Church, to say that we are sorry.

We tell God that we are sorry.

We tell one another that we are sorry.

We ask God to help us be like Jesus.

We say, "We are sorry, Lord,

✛ for the times we did not show love,

✛ for the times we hurt others,

✛ for the times we did not obey, and

✛ for the times we were selfish."

We Come to Our Good Shepherd CHAPTER 18 123

Turn your book upside down.

You will see how we feel when we are forgiven.

We Remember

What do we do when we have not shown love?

When we have not shown love, we say, "I'm sorry."

We Respond

Jesus, forgive me.

Jesus' Two Great Commandments

1. Love God.
2. Love others.

Put 1 in the circle if the picture shows how we love God.

Put 2 in the circle if the picture shows how we love others.

Draw your favorite part of the story of the lost sheep.

No2

We Come to Our Good Shepherd

Greeting

Leader: May the love and care of Jesus, our Good Shepherd, be with us as we gather today to celebrate Jesus' loving forgiveness. Let us pray to him now.

Prayer

Reading

(adapted from Luke 15:4–7)

Reader 1: A reading from the Gospel of Luke:

Reader 2: A shepherd has 100 beautiful sheep. One wanders away. The shepherd leaves the other 99 sheep. He goes out to find the one that is lost. When he finds it, he is so happy that he hugs it. He carries it home in his arms. Then he calls his friends together, and says,

Reader 3: "I am so happy that I found my lost lamb. Let's celebrate!"

Reader 1: In the same way, heaven is filled with joy when one person says, "I am sorry."

Examination of Conscience

Leader: Now I have some questions for you to think about. They help us see how well we are following Jesus.

Expression of Sorrow

Response: We are sorry, Lord, and we come now to you.

Prayer

Leader: Jesus, our Good Shepherd, looks for us when we stray from goodness. He is always ready to forgive us when we are sorry. May almighty God have mercy on us, forgive us our sins, and bring us to everlasting life.

All: Amen.

Leader: Go now in love and peace to follow our Good Shepherd.

Song

Jesus is our Good Shepherd.

He guides us.

He cares for us.

Jesus is our Good Shepherd.

We love and follow him.

Cultivating a Caring Heart

Isn't it wonderful to be loved? The human heart yearns to be seen, known, and loved. When we experience the rush of joy that comes from knowing we are loved for who we most truly are, we long to spread that joy and deep gladness with others.

Your child has been learning about God's love and goodness in Unit 3. God is the one who sees us, knows us, and loves us better than anyone else. God loves us even in our moments of vulnerability and human failure. When we come to know and accept this love, we respond by loving God in return and by acting on the desire to share that love with others.

Jesus summed up this idea when he responded to a request to name the greatest commandment: "You shall love the Lord, your God, with all your heart, with all your soul, and with all your mind. This is the greatest and the first commandment. The second is like it: You shall love your neighbor as yourself." (Matthew 22:37–39) It is God's love of us that helps create in us a caring heart. As the first nurturers of the faith, you have been given a sacred trust to cultivate your child's caring heart. Fortunately, family life offers many ordinary opportunities to cultivate both your own and your child's caring heart.

Family Feature

Recognize the ways the people in your family are already loving and serving others. Together as a family, draw a picture depicting a scene in which the members of your family are helping one another—perhaps by making dinner, cleaning the house, putting away personal items, and so on. Think of actual ways you show your love by the things you do at home to help one another. (Suggestion: You can draw one single scene, or draw two lines to create four equal-sized boxes and draw four scenes.)

The Key: Do Everything with a Loving Heart

We all know that it matters what attitude and energy we bring to a task or project. Think about the difference between the sales clerk who warmly greets you and attends to you right away, versus the one who barely acknowledges your existence and goes through the motions of serving you as if he or she were sleepwalking. It's not only what we do, but the attitude, intention, and energy we bring to what we do that makes the difference.

You can experience a profound improvement in your level of satisfaction and joy in life by simply doing everything you are called upon to do during the day in a spirit of great love. Works done with a grateful spirit are acts of generous caring, not dreary obligations. Blessed Teresa of Calcutta, who lived a life of heroic holiness, advised, "We cannot all do great things, but we can do small things with great love." Living in a family involves doing many small things every day. When you approach these tasks—cleaning the house, paying the bills, making meals—with a heart full of love, your whole outlook changes. Your child is capable of growing in his or her capacity to take this same approach to the day as well.

When our hearts are open to others, we have countless opportunities to serve. This lesson of the heart is perhaps the most important one for your child to learn about loving our neighbors.

Begin each day being mindful of the choice we have: to live mainly for ourselves or to care for others. You might say this prayer with your child each day:

Dear God,
Thank you for loving us on good days and bad days, on happy days and sad days, in sunshine and in rain. Lead us to love others as you love us. Give us the joy of sharing your love with the people we will meet today. We ask this in Jesus' name. Amen.

Family Feature

Here are some ways to nurture the naturally loving heart of your child:

Nurture your child's empathy, which is the building block of moral growth. Being aware of and caring about others is our invitation to get beyond self-absorption and to serve others. You can cultivate your child's empathy when you read books or watch TV. Occasionally during the action of the plot, ask your child, "How do you think that person felt when (describe what just happened)?" For a great book on learning empathy as the basis of friendship, read with your child *George and Martha: The Complete Stories of Two Best Friends* by James Marshall and Maurice Sendak. It's about two hilarious hippos who learn some of the same lessons your child is learning.

Build on your child's natural sense of fairness. First graders have a developing sense of what's fair and what's not. Respecting their sense of what's fair while helping them recognize how fairness extends to their siblings, playmates, and even parents builds a solid foundation for later lessons about fairness on the community level and beyond.

Model an orientation toward others in your home by demonstrating a willingness to acknowledge and respond to the needs of people beyond your family. This shows itself in concrete efforts such as helping a neighbor in need, volunteering at the local community center, or coaching a youth athletic team. You are showing your child how to live. Specifically you can

- *get involved in projects to serve others.* When your parish has a food drive or a program to gather gifts for those in need, get your child involved. Let him or her help select what's to be given and help you bring it to the designated collection center.

- *keep it fun.* Model that giving can be done with a joyful heart.

- *work with others.* Children not only like to be involved with other children, it is good for them to watch adults go out of their way to help others. Joining with others in service projects is a great way to show your child, "This is what adult believers do."

It can be tempting for parents to think of their children, especially when they are young, as recipients of our love and service. And that is good. A solid foundation of having their needs met is a wonderful gift we give our children. But our children also have a great need to become loving and caring people in this world. As parents it is crucial that we not only model that behavior but give them age-appropriate opportunities as they grow to love and serve other people. In that way, you cultivate the loving heart that your child was created to bring to the world.

Visit **www.christourlife.org/family** for more family resources.

Jesus Shows His Great Love

An angel said to Mary Magdalene, Mary the mother of James, and Salome: "You seek Jesus of Nazareth, the crucified. He has been raised. He is not here. Go and tell his disciples and Peter: 'You will find him in Galilee just as Jesus told you.'"

adapted from Mark 16:6–7

A Letter Home

Dear Parents and Family,

A central mystery lies at the heart of our Catholic faith. That mystery is revealed in the suffering, death, and Resurrection of Jesus, by which he reconciled the human family to God. We call this the Paschal, or Easter, Mystery.

In Unit 4 the children learn about that mystery and how Jesus remains with us today through the Holy Spirit. They also explore the beginnings of the Church, its mission to spread the Gospel, and Mary's place as the Mother of the Church. The children learn that the Holy Spirit leads us to become holy in our own daily lives. Time you spend with your child reviewing and praying over this material will help you take in these truths and make them your own.

Key points explored in the unit include:

> **In each Mass, Christ is truly present to nourish us with the Eucharist and to make us all one with each other and with God.**

> **Jesus models a new way to respond to misunderstanding, envy, jealousy, and other sufferings. He responds with confidence that God's ways lead to fullness of life.**

> **When Jesus was raised from the dead, a new light shone through the darkness and overcame sin and death. The children are taught to associate Easter with signs of new life and the experience of peace and joy because our risen Lord remains with us.**

> **The Holy Spirit is available to each one of us throughout our lives to help us grow in holiness and virtue.**

> **Mary is a courageous model of faithfulness whose yes to God can inspire all of us to respond generously and faithfully to God by serving others.**

> **The children learn that their good deeds give glory to the Father, Son, and Holy Spirit. They prepare to welcome the Lord into every moment of the day.**

Chapters 19–24 each end with a review and a Building Family Faith handout, which the children will bring home. This handout gives you a quick review of what your child learned and offers practical ways to reinforce the lesson. At the end of the unit, the children will bring home a Family Feature handout to help nurture the family's faith at home.

Jesus Gives the Gift of Himself

Palm Sunday

Have you ever seen a parade?

People march and bands play.

We wave flags and cheer.

Long ago a parade honored Jesus.

People put their cloaks on the street.

Jesus rode along the street on a donkey.

People waved palm branches.

They shouted "Hosanna" to Jesus.

They wanted to make Jesus king.

Holy Week is a special time for God's family, the Church.

The Church remembers important happenings in Jesus' life.

On Palm Sunday the Church remembers the parade that honored Jesus.

Complete each sentence. Draw a line to the correct word.

Jesus is our _____ .   ●   ● branches

We pray and sing to _____ . ●   ● Sunday

We carry palm _____ .   ●   ● king

It is Palm _____ .   ●   ● Jesus

Holy Thursday

Gifts are a part of celebrations.

There are birthday gifts, Christmas gifts, and going-away gifts.

A gift is a way of showing love.

Write the words to complete the story.

The night before he died, Jesus celebrated

a meal with his friends.

At this last supper, he gave all his friends a gift.

The gift was himself.

_____

Jesus took _____ .
                              bread

He said, "This is my body."

_____

He took a cup of _____ .
                                    wine

He said, "This is my blood."

Jesus gave the gift of himself to his friends.

He told them,

   "Do this in memory of me."

Luke 22:19

We Celebrate Jesus' Gift of Himself at Mass

At the Last Supper, Jesus offered himself to the Father.

Then he gave us the gift of himself.

We celebrate his gift at Mass.

At Mass the priest says what Jesus said.

"This is my Body. This is my Blood."

_____

The Body and Blood of _____ is God's gift to us.
                              Jesus

God's people receive this gift of Jesus in Holy Communion.

Jesus is present as the Bread of Life.

We belong to God's people.

We will receive Jesus in a special way in Holy Communion.

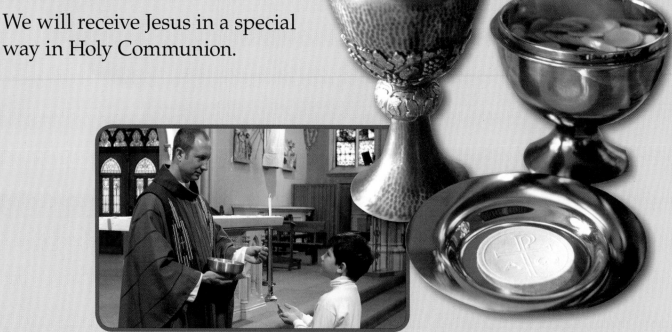

At Mass with My Family and Friends

Draw a picture of a priest at an altar. Draw bread and a cup on the altar. Draw yourself standing at the altar with your family and friends.

Good Friday

Jesus died on the cross for us.

Jesus showed how much he loved his Father.

He showed how much God loves us.

Jesus gave his life for us.

On the cross, he gave us Mary for a mother.

Jesus died and rose to free us from sin.

Now we have new life.

We can bring Jesus' love to our world.

We can be happy in heaven forever.

A Moment with Jesus

Pray the words you wrote. Thank Jesus for saving us.

Write the prayer.

_____

- - - - - - - - - - - - - - - - -

_____

I love you,

- - - - - - - - - - - - - - - - -

_____

Jesus

_____

- - - - - - - - - - - - - - - - -

_____

my Savior.

Match each day with the correct picture.

Palm Sunday ● ●

Holy Thursday ● ●

Good Friday ● ●

We Remember

What gift does Jesus give us at Mass?

Jesus gives us the gift of himself at Mass.

Why is Jesus our Savior?

Jesus is our Savior because he died and rose to save us from sin and bring us new life.

We Respond

Give thanks to the LORD, for he is good. His love lasts forever.

adapted from Psalm 118:1

Building Family Faith

JESUS CONTINUES TO be present to us today. He is present in a special way at Mass. At the Last Supper, Jesus gave his Body and Blood to his friends. At Mass we receive Jesus' Body and Blood in Holy Communion. At each Mass Jesus offers himself to the Father, just as he did on Good Friday. We give thanks and praise to Jesus in the Mass. It is a time of great celebration.

REFLECT

Then he took the bread, said the blessing, broke it, and gave it to them, saying, "This is my body, which will be given for you; do this in memory of me." And likewise the cup after they had eaten, saying, "This cup is the new covenant in my blood, which will be shed for you."

Luke 22:19–20

DISCUSS AS A FAMILY

- Why is it important to go to Mass?
- How is the Mass like a family meal?

PRAY

O Christ, by your holy cross, you have redeemed the world.

DO

Make plans to attend the Holy Thursday Mass as a family.

Visit **www.christourlife.org/family** for more family resources.

Jesus Is Risen

Birds sing.

Flowers bloom.

Bunnies hop.

New life is everywhere.

Easter

Jesus Is Risen

New life in the spring reminds us of Jesus' new life.

He rose from the dead on **Easter** Sunday with new life!

This is called the **Resurrection** of Jesus.

After the Resurrection, Jesus had a glorified body.

He visited his friends.

Alleluia

The risen Jesus is with us today.

He is with us in the **Eucharist**.

He is with us in all things that are good and beautiful.

He brings new life to those who believe in him.

The Road to Emmaus

Two friends of Jesus did not know that he had risen.

They were sad.

While they were walking down a road, a kind man met them.

He asked, "Why are you sad?"

"Jesus has died," they told him.

The man said, "Jesus had to die to bring new life."

The two friends asked the kind man to stay with them.

At supper he blessed the bread, broke it, and gave it to the friends.

Then they knew that the man was Jesus.

How happy they were!

Trace the bread and color it.

Jesus, our risen Savior, is with us.

These pictures show where we can meet Jesus.

Connect the dots.

Jesus visited his apostles on Easter evening.

He said, "Peace be with you. If you forgive people's sins, they are forgiven."

Jesus gives peace to his friends. He wants his friends to bring peace to others.

How can you bring Jesus' peace to someone today?

Is the child in each picture giving peace?

Write yes or no.

"You can't play with my game."

_____

_____

"Dad, would you like to see the paper?"

_____

_____

"That was a good dinner, Mom."

_____

_____

"Let me help you find the pictures."

_____

_____

For Jesus

Write the word pray.

Read the sentence.

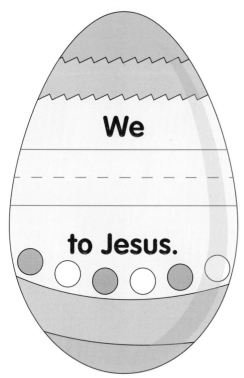

We

to Jesus.

For Others

Write the word peace.

Read the sentence.

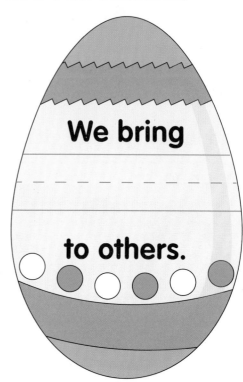

We bring

to others.

Complete each sentence with the correct letter.

1. The Last Supper was on _____.

2. Jesus changed bread and wine into _____.

3. Jesus shared the bread and wine with _____.

4. At Mass priests act and speak for _____.

5. At Mass God's people receive the _____ of Jesus.

6. On Easter Jesus gave us the gift of _____.

7. Jesus died to save us from _____.

8. Jesus rose from the dead on _____.

A. Jesus

B. himself

C. his apostles

D. Holy Thursday

E. sin

F. Easter Sunday

G. Body and Blood

H. peace

Pray these words adapted from the Peace Prayer of Saint Francis.

Lord, make me an instrument of your peace:

where there is hatred, let me bring love;

where there is injury, let me bring pardon;

where there is doubt, let me bring faith;

where there is despair, let me bring hope;

where there is darkness, let me bring light;

and where there is sadness, let me bring joy.

Pray about these pictures.

We Remember

When did Jesus rise from the dead?

Jesus rose from the dead on Easter Sunday.

Words to Know

Easter   **Eucharist**

Resurrection

We Respond

Alleluia! Jesus is risen and is with us.

Building Family Faith

YOUR CHILD IS learning about Jesus' Resurrection and about the ways that Jesus is still with us. Jesus rose from the dead on Easter Sunday and appeared to many of his disciples, including Thomas, who doubted that he had risen. Jesus is still present in the world—in the Eucharist, in the Church, and in the lives of his friends.

REFLECT

"And it happened that, while he was with them at table, he took bread, said the blessing, broke it, and gave it to them. With that their eyes were opened and they recognized him, but he vanished from their sight."

Luke 24:30–31

DISCUSS AS A FAMILY

Share ideas about the many ways that we are reminded of Jesus' presence—at home, in school, in our community, among our friends, in the parish, and at work.

PRAY

Lord Jesus, open my eyes to see you.

DO

Make family preparations for an Easter celebration to honor the risen Jesus.

Visit **www.christourlife.org/family** for more family resources.

Jesus Sends Us the Spirit

Jesus Returns to His Father

Jesus and his apostles were on a mountain. He said to them,

"Go and baptize all people.
Teach them everything I told you.
I am with you always.
I will send the Holy Spirit."

Jesus returned to his Father.

His friends no longer saw him.

The apostles went back to the city.

They prayed for the **Holy Spirit** to come.

147

Jesus Sends the Holy Spirit

The apostles waited and prayed.

Jesus' mother, Mary, was with them.

They heard a strong wind.

They saw tongues of fire.

Color the tongues of fire.

They knew God was there.

Jesus kept his promise.

He sent the Holy Spirit.

Mary and the apostles were filled with the Holy Spirit.

The Holy Spirit Is God

The Holy Spirit filled the apostles' hearts with love.

He helped the apostles begin God's new family, the Church.

The Holy Spirit made the apostles loving and brave.

They had the strength to go out and tell people about Jesus' great love.

The Holy Spirit is with us too.

He helps us show everyone that Jesus loves us all.

Jesus Gave Us Special Gifts at Baptism

At your Baptism, you were filled with God's grace.

God gave you new life.

The Holy Spirit came to live within you.

You became God's child and a member of God's family.

God also gave you special gifts called virtues.

Virtues help you live as God's child. Here are three special virtues:

faith　　　**hope**　　　**love**

A Moment with Jesus

Thank Jesus for the gifts of faith, hope, and love.

Draw a line from each word to the correct symbol and meaning.

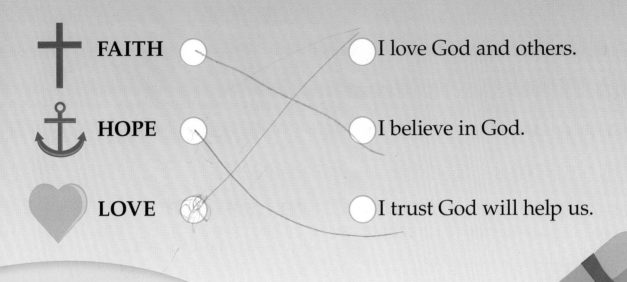

FAITH ⚪ — ⚪ I love God and others.

HOPE ⚪ — ⚪ I believe in God.

LOVE ⚪ — ⚪ I trust God will help us.

Put the three virtues into action. Write what you can do.

Because I have faith, I _believe in god_ .

Because I have hope, I _trust god will help us_ .

Because I have love, I _love god and others_ .

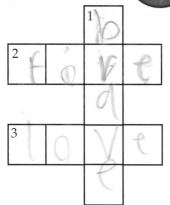

Word Bank

love

brave

fire

Use the clues to work this puzzle.

Across

2. It was above the head of Mary and each apostle.

3. The Holy Spirit filled the hearts of the apostles with it.

Down

1. The Holy Spirit helped the apostles feel this way.

We Remember

Who is the Holy Spirit?

The Holy Spirit is God. He was sent by Jesus and the Father.

Word to Know

Holy Spirit

We Respond

Come, Holy Spirit! Fill my heart with Jesus' love.

Building Family Faith

GOD IS PRESENT in our lives and in our world through the Holy Spirit. After he went to be with the Father, Jesus sent the Holy Spirit to his apostles. The Holy Spirit has been with us ever since. We receive the Holy Spirit at Baptism. Through the Spirit we know the Father and the Son. The Spirit is present in our family, our parish, and our Church.

REFLECT

[Jesus] said to them again, "Peace be with you. As the Father has sent me, so I send you." And when he had said this, he breathed on them and said to them, "Receive the holy Spirit."

John 20:21–22

DISCUSS AS A FAMILY

• We cannot see the Holy Spirit. Talk about other important things that are real, but that we cannot see.

• Discuss times when we thought God was giving us special help to deal with difficult situations.

PRAY

Come, Holy Spirit, fill our hearts with your love.

DO

At bedtime, make the Sign of the Cross with your child. Mention that we have learned that God is Father, Son, and Holy Spirit.

Visit **www.christourlife.org/family** for more family resources.

Jesus Is with Us in His Church

The Church Is God's Family

God's big Christian family is called the Church.

All baptized people belong to it.

The Holy Spirit is with the Church.

The Holy Spirit helps Christians bring Jesus' love to the world.

Jesus Chose a Leader for His Church

Before Jesus went to heaven, he spoke to Peter.

He said, "Do you love me?"

Peter said, "Yes, Lord, you know that I love you."

Jesus said, "Feed my sheep."

adapted from John 21:17

Jesus told Peter to care for his family, the Church.

Then he made Peter the leader of the Church.

Peter was the first **pope**.

The Pope Leads the Church Today

The Church has a pope today.

He acts for Jesus on earth.

We call him the Holy Father.

The pope and the other bishops lead **Catholics** in spreading Jesus' love.

A Moment with Jesus

Pray for all the leaders of our Church.

We Belong to the Catholic Church

The priest who baptized you said,

> "[Your name], I baptize you in
> the name of the Father, and of
> the Son, and of the Holy Spirit."

We joined the Catholic Church when we were baptized.

We became Catholics.

The Catholic family welcomed us into the Church.

Jesus invites all people to belong to his Church.

Color the banner.

Complete this family tree.

Write the names of people who belong to God's family.

parents

Ants kincles

grandparents

cousins

sister

pets jesus

god parents

God jesus

God's Family

Draw yourself at Mass.

We Remember

To what Church do you belong?
I belong to the Catholic Church.
I am a Catholic.

Words to Know

Catholic   pope

We Respond

Lord Jesus, help me be a good Catholic.

Building Family Faith

YOUR CHILD IS learning about the Church—the family of faith that carries the Good News of Jesus to the world. Your child is part of this worldwide body. People of all races, cultures, and languages belong to the Church. We are all one body, united by our love for Christ and our desire to do his work. The visible sign of our unity is the pope, the head of the Church.

REFLECT
"Go, therefore, and make disciples of all nations, baptizing them in the name of the Father, and of the Son, and of the holy Spirit, teaching them to observe all that I have commanded you. And behold, I am with you always, until the end of the age."

Matthew 28:19–20

Visit **www.christourlife.org/family** for more family resources.

DISCUSS AS A FAMILY
Talk about your experiences of the larger Church: images and articles about the pope, other Church leaders, and Christians in other countries.

PRAY
Bless your Church, Lord. Protect it. Make it strong.

DO
Do a family project on the pope. Find pictures of him. Find out what he said at recent celebrations and discuss his words.

Mary Is the Mother of the Church

Mary Is Our Mother

Jesus gave us his mother to be our mother too.

Mary is the Mother of the Church.

She always listened to God.

We call her our Blessed Mother.

Mary Is Our Queen

One day Jesus took Mary, body and soul, to heaven.

He made her Queen of Heaven.

Now Mary prays for us and helps us be like Jesus.

We love Mary and honor her.

We try to be kind and loving as she is.

Jesus will take us to heaven someday if we follow him.

Then we will live forever with Jesus, Mary, the saints, and the angels.

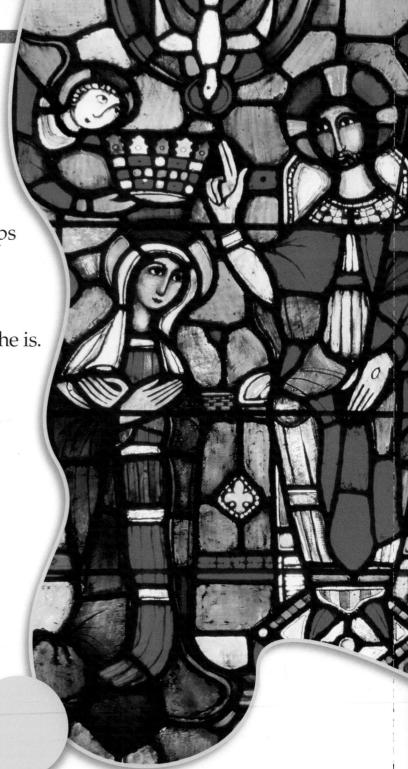

A Moment with Jesus

Pray to Jesus in the quiet of your heart. Tell Jesus how you will be like Mary his mother.

Draw yourself bringing flowers to Mary.

Immaculate Mary,
your praises we sing.
You reign now in splendor
with Jesus our King.

Ave, ave, ave Maria!
Ave, ave, Maria!

Mary Helps Us Be Good Christians

Mary is a good role model.

She shows us how to be good Christians.

She shows us how to be like Jesus.

She helps us be holy.

How does Mary help us be holy?

Complete each sentence about how Mary helps us be holy. **Use the word bank.**

1. Have _____ faith _____ in God.

2. Say _____ yes _____ to God.

3. _____ Love _____ God and others.

4. Do _____ good _____ and stay away from sin.

good	yes	faith	love

Saint Thérèse Loved Mary

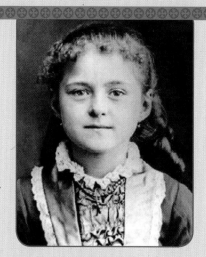

Many saints looked to Mary for help.

Saint Thérèse was one of them.

She asked Mary to help her be more like Jesus.

She showed us how to honor Mary.

Draw a picture of how you honor Mary.

Connect the dots to make a gift for Mary. Color the gift.

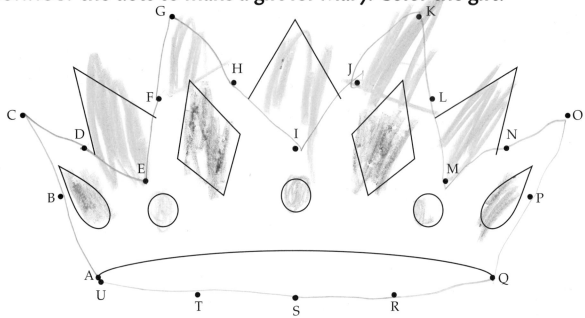

Mary, Queen of Heaven!

We Remember

Who is Mary?

Mary is God's Mother and our mother and queen.

We Respond

O my Queen, O my Mother, I love you and give myself to you.

Building Family Faith

MARY HAS A special place of honor in the Church. Because she is the mother of Jesus, she is the mother of the Church, which carries on Jesus' work. That means she is the spiritual mother for your child and for all who share in Jesus' life through Baptism. Mary cares for us as a mother. We can turn to her in prayer. We can ask her to help us in times of need.

REFLECT

When Jesus saw his mother and the disciple there whom he loved, he said to his mother, "Woman, behold, your son." Then he said to the disciple, "Behold, your mother." And from that hour the disciple took her into his home.

John 19:26–27

DISCUSS AS A FAMILY

• What does a mother do for her family?

• What problems can Mary our mother in heaven help us with?

PRAY

Holy Mary, Mother of God, pray for us.

DO

At bedtime, ask your child to mention a special need he or she has. Pray three Hail Marys for this intention.

Visit **www.christourlife.org/family** for more family resources.

The Holy Spirit Helps the Church

The Holy Spirit Helps Us Know Jesus Through the Gospels

The Holy Spirit helped the apostles teach people about Jesus.

He helped people write the **Gospels** of Matthew, Mark, Luke, and John.

The Gospels are part of the Bible.

They tell the Good News that Jesus loves and saved us.

The Holy Spirit helps us listen to the Gospel at Mass.

He helps us listen when the priest tells us about Jesus.

The Holy Spirit helps us be like Jesus.

The Holy Spirit Helped the First Christians

Long ago the Holy Spirit helped the Church.

He helped the first Christians love God and others.

He helped them pray and share.

The Holy Spirit helps us be good Christians today.

He helps us love God and others.

He helps us pray and share.

Love is the badge of a Catholic.

Trace the words on the badge.

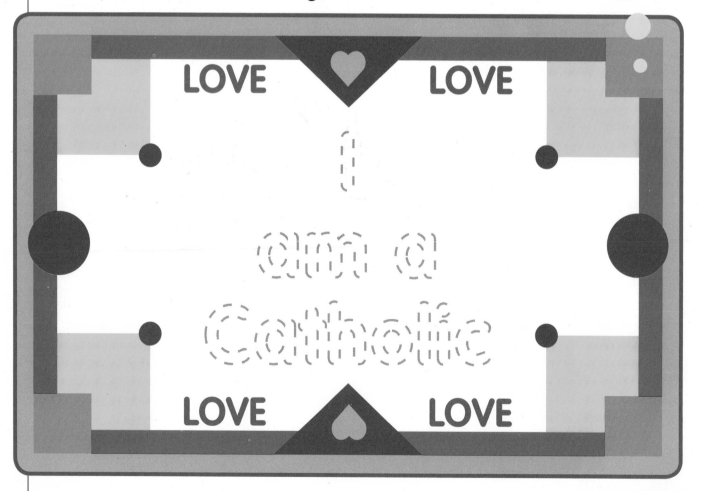

The Holy Spirit Helps Us Be a Light

Light shines.

Jesus said,

> "You are the light of the world."
>
> Matthew 5:14

Jesus wants us to let God's goodness shine out from us.

The Holy Spirit helps us spread the Good News of Jesus.

We can help people we meet know Jesus.

We can help people in mission lands know Jesus.

We can pray that many will join God's family, the Church.

Write what you can do to show how your light shines.

The Holy Spirit Helped Saint Martin Show Love

Martin was a young man from Tours, France.

He heard about Jesus' teaching on love.

One day he met a man.

It was very cold.

The man had no warm clothes.

He was cold and shivering.

Martin remembered what Jesus said about love.

Martin cut his cloak in two.

He gave half to the man.

That night Martin saw Jesus in a dream.

Jesus was wearing the cloak Martin gave the man.

Draw yourself bringing Jesus' love to someone you know.

Write the person's name below.

_____

I can bring Jesus' love to _____ .

A Moment with Jesus

Ask Jesus to bless this person.

Write the Good News about Jesus.

We Remember

Who helps us spread the Good News of Jesus' love?

The Holy Spirit helps us spread the Good News of Jesus' love.

Word to Know

Gospel

We Respond

Holy Spirit, help me spread Jesus' love.

Building Family Faith

THE MOST IMPORTANT work of the Church is spreading the Good News of God's love for people everywhere. We do this primarily by acts of love. The first Christians were known as people who loved one another. That's how Catholics today should be known—as people who love. Catholics are people of loving hearts, loving words, and loving deeds.

REFLECT
"Just so, your light must shine before others, that they may see your good deeds and glorify your heavenly Father."

Matthew 5:16

DISCUSS AS A FAMILY
• How have people in your family acted lovingly toward each other?

• How has your family helped others—in the neighborhood, in your extended family, at school, in the parish, or in volunteer work?

PRAY
Lord, show us how to love.

DO
Review what your family has been doing to help others. Ask if there is more that the Lord wants you to do.

Visit **www.christourlife.org/family** for more family resources.

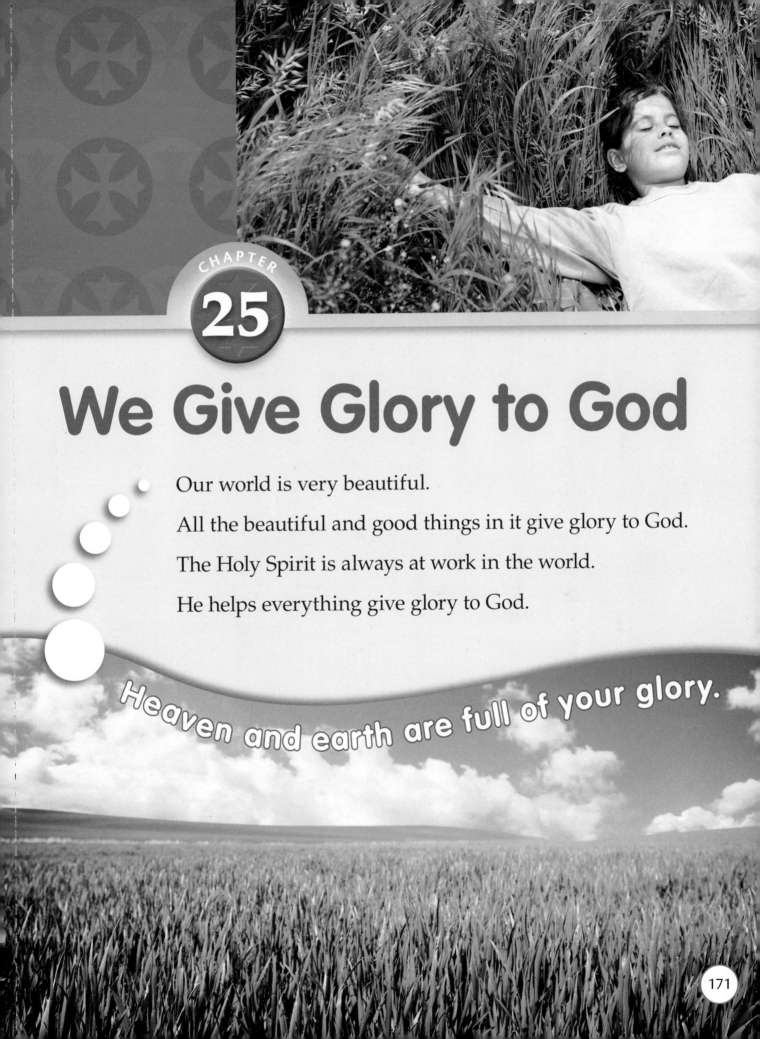

We Give Glory to God

Our world is very beautiful.

All the beautiful and good things in it give glory to God.

The Holy Spirit is always at work in the world.

He helps everything give glory to God.

Heaven and earth are full of your glory.

The Holy Spirit helps us give glory to God.

We praise the three Persons in one God when we pray.

This prayer is called the Glory Be to the Father.

Glory be to the Father,
and to the Son,
and to the Holy Spirit.
As it was in the beginning,
is now, and ever shall be,
world without end.

Amen.

Kind words give glory to God.

Write the missing letters to complete the words.

"May I _h_ _____ ?"

"I _l_ _____ you."

"Come and _p_ _____ ."

"I am _s_ _____ ."

Good actions give glory to God. We give glory to God

• when we obey him and our parents.
• when we help others.
• when we sing, laugh, and play.
• when we help make our world beautiful.

Draw a picture of yourself giving glory to God.

Jesus said he would always be with us.

Jesus is with us in the Holy Spirit.

He will be with us this summer.

We can help others know that

We can help our world give glory to God.

Trace the letters. Then color the words.

Color the banner.

JOY
is ours when we give glory to God.

We Remember

Why do we give glory to God?
We give glory to God because he is good and he made us.

We Respond

Glory Be to the Father, and to the Son, and to the Holy Spirit.

Trinity Activities

Use the clues to work the puzzle.

Word Bank
Father
Son
Holy Spirit

Across

2. our Helper in living the Gospel

Down

1. our Creator

3. our Savior Jesus Christ

Unscramble the words to find two prayers that give glory to the Trinity.

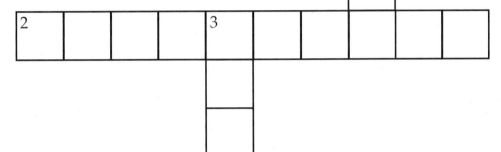

g n i S   f o   h e t   s r o C s

y l r o G   e B   o t   h e t   e F t a h r

The Christian Family Album

Priest

Christians

Pope

Mary

Peter Luke Matthew Mark John

Jesus

Holy Spirit

Sister

Apostles

The Church is God's big, loving Christian family.

Some of God's family are already with him in heaven.

Tell something about each picture in the Christian Family Album.

We Celebrate

We Give Glory to God

Song

Leader: Today we are doing what the angels and saints do in heaven. We are praising God. We are giving glory to God, who is with us always.

Reading (adapted from 1 Corinthians 10:31)

Reader 1: A reading from the First Letter of Paul to the Corinthians

Reader 2: "Whether you eat or drink, or whatever you do, do everything for the glory of God."

The Word of the Lord.

All: Thanks be to God.

Silent Prayer

Spontaneous Prayer

Leader: We are made to give glory to God. We can give God glory by everything we do. Let's tell God some of these ways. The response will be "Glory to God."

All: Glory to God.

Glory Be to the Father

Leader: Let us pray the Glory Be to the Father together.

All: Glory be to the Father,

and to the Son,

and to the Holy Spirit.

As it was in the beginning, is now, and ever shall be,

world without end.

Amen.

Song

God the Father, God the Son,

Holy Spirit — all are one.

Come and live in us we pray,

Stay with us both night and day.

Thank you for your life and love,

And all your blessings from above.

Family Feature

Discovering God in Your Home

"I am the vine, you are the branches. Whoever remains in me and I in him will bear much fruit."

John 15:5

Do you ever feel that God is far away? Jesus was eager to tell his disciples that the exact opposite is true. How close is God to us? Jesus explained it this way. He said, "I am the vine and you are the branches." If you look closely at a vine, you'll have a hard time seeing where the vine leaves off and the branches begin. What's more, the very life that sustains the vine flows out and through the branches so that they might bear fruit for the world. God is as close to us as a vine is to its branches, as a breath is to the one who breathes. And the life of God flows through us when we are open to receiving it and sharing it.

We know how that feels—having the life of God flowing through us. We feel it when we are freely generous and help someone in need. We feel it when we get past a difficult time with a family member and feel reconciled and loving once more. We feel it when we spend time in prayer and experience deeply that God loves us more than we can know.

God wants us to share in that divine life. He sent his Son, Jesus, to bring that life to us. Jesus promised his disciples and he promises us that he will remain with us for all our days. That means through good days and bad days, disappointing days and satisfying days, days we feel like great parents and days we feel that we can't do a single thing right. Jesus is present for us, and his life and love can flow through us into our family, and that love can bear great fruit. That is his promise to us.

Family Feature

Where is Jesus present to your family? Here are a few places to look.

- **At church**—As Catholics we believe that Jesus is present in a very special way in the Eucharist. The bread and the wine become the Body and Blood of Christ. We believe that we, the people assembled for worship, become the Body of Christ as well. We also encounter Jesus in the reading of Sacred Scripture and in the fellowship we share with our fellow parishioners before and after Mass.

- **At work**—The work you do is meant to be holy. Of course it's a good thing to make a living and support our families. But all work, whether paid or unpaid, when done for the glory of God and for the common good, is blessed. As lay people, our job is to bring Christ into the world. We do that when we contribute to and help fashion a social system based on justice for all and when we participate in the community of our fellow workers with respect, dignity, and charity.

- **At home**—Daily family life is filled with opportunities to encounter Jesus. When asked what was required to get to heaven, Jesus told the crowds to feed the hungry and give drink to the thirsty. He said that whenever we do that for those in need, we will be feeding and tending to Jesus himself. We parents have ample opportunities to tend to the needs of other family members. We can be mindful that in doing so we are serving Jesus. Plus, Jesus promised that whenever two or more are gathered in his name he is among them. So whenever we pray as a family, we can be confident that Jesus is right there with us.

The Spirit in Your Home

Before Jesus ascended into heaven, he promised to send the Holy Spirit to guide us. The Holy Spirit comes to us bearing gifts, so we need to be on the lookout for them. Here's some help.

 Have you intuitively known how to handle a tough situation in your family? That's **wisdom**.

 Have you stopped yourself from getting angry with your child long enough to think about what it feels like to be in his or her shoes? That's **understanding**.

 Have you clearly and firmly stated your beliefs about right and wrong to someone in your family? That's **counsel**.

 Have you hung in there when you wanted to throw in the towel? That's **fortitude**.

 Are you open-minded, letting go of superstitions, prejudices, and small-mindedness? That's **knowledge**.

 Do you realize you need God's help and that all life is a gift? That's **piety**.

 Have you felt awe—perhaps the first time you held your child in your arms? That's **fear of the Lord**.

These are the gifts of the Holy Spirit, signs that God's love is flowing through your life and in your home. The gifts are yours; look for them.

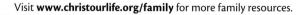
Visit **www.christourlife.org/family** for more family resources.

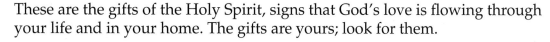

Family Feature

Stay Connected!

Jesus says that he is the vine that gives us life. If we stay connected to him, we will bear great fruit, which means we will do many good things in our lives. Gather the family together and have family members write in each grape a loving or kind act that shows God's love. These are just some of the signs of God's presence in our homes.

Special Seasons and Lessons

The Year in Our Church

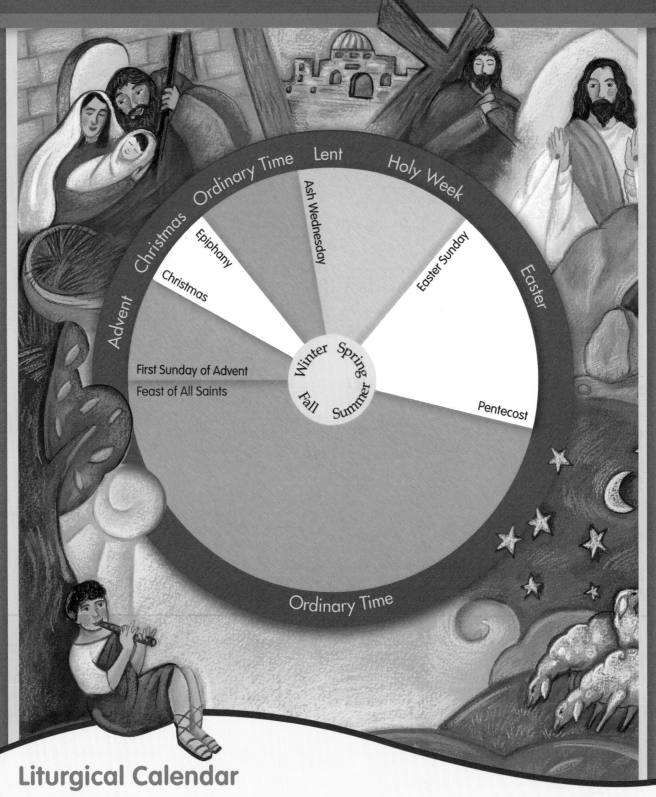

Winter
Spring
Summer
Fall

Advent
Christmas
Ordinary Time
Lent
Holy Week

Epiphany
Christmas
Ash Wednesday
Easter Sunday
Easter

First Sunday of Advent
Feast of All Saints
Pentecost
Ordinary Time

Liturgical Calendar

The liturgical calendar shows the feast days and seasons of the Church year. The different colors stand for the many seasons.

1 | Feast of All Saints

A saint is a person who loved God on earth. Saints live with God in heaven.

Saints help us to live and love like Jesus. We learn about the saints and ask them to pray for us.

On All Saints Day, we honor all the saints living with God in heaven.

God calls all of us to be saints. We are happy when we live in God's love.

Procession of the Rosario Virgen in Fuengirola Malaga, Andalusia Spain

Patron Saints

We can ask our patron saint to help us to love God better.

A patron saint cares for and prays for a person or group in a special way. Everyone has a patron saint.

Write the name of a saint you want to pray for you.

Saint _____ , pray for us.

Saint Frances Cabrini   Saint John   Saint Julie   Saint Joseph

Draw a picture of how you will show your love for God as the saints did.

2 | Advent

During Advent, we prepare to celebrate Jesus' birth at Christmas.

We remember that God keeps his promises.

We remember that God sent his Son, Jesus, to be our Savior.

We remember that Jesus is still with us today.

We look forward to the day when Jesus will come again in glory.

Advent Wreath

Write the prayer.

_____

- -

_____

Come, Lord Jesus.

Color the wreath green.

Color one candle pink and the others purple.

Draw a flame on one candle each week of Advent.

3 | Christmas

Come, let us adore him.

Song "O Come, All Ye Faithful"
O come, let us adore him,
O come, let us adore him,
O come, let us adore him,
Christ the Lord.

Reading A reading from the Gospel according to Luke.
Mary and Joseph went to Bethlehem.
They looked for a room.
There was no room anywhere.
They went to a stable.
There Jesus was born.
Mary laid him in a manger.

adapted from Luke 2:1–7

The Word of the Lord.

All: Thanks be to God.

Song "Happy Birthday, Dear Jesus"

Prayer

Response: Glory to you, O God!

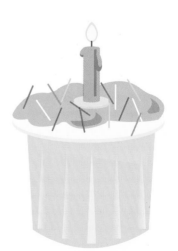

Reading   A reading from the Gospel according to Luke.
An angel came to the shepherds.
He said, "Jesus is born.
He is in Bethlehem.
He is lying in a manger."
Angels sang, "Glory to God."
The shepherds went quickly to see Jesus.
How happy they were!

adapted from Luke 2:8–16

The Word of the Lord.

All: Thanks be to God.

Prayer

Response: We thank you, God our Father!

Song   "Silent Night"

4 | Lent

Lent is a time for us to grow. We remember Jesus' death. We celebrate his new life. We prepare for Easter.

Lent begins on **Ash Wednesday**. It lasts for 40 days.

During Lent, the priest blesses ashes and traces the Sign of the Cross on our foreheads.

We think about Jesus' love for us. We show our love for God and for others.

A Time to Grow and Change

Connect the dotted lines and see the surprise.
Color the surprise.
The caterpillar has a new life.

Follow the numbers.
Color a caterpillar or a leaf each day
you do something to show your love.

40 Holy Saturday

39 Good Friday

37

34

35

32

36

33

31

30

29

38 Holy Thursday

15

14

16

18

28

27

26

13

12

17

10

20

25

19

22

24

11

8

9

21

23

7

6

5

3

4

Watch the caterpillar grow and change.

We can change too.

We want to grow to be more like Jesus during Lent.

2

1 Ash Wednesday

5 | Holy Week

During Lent we get ready for Easter. Easter is the holiest day of the year. The week before Easter is called **Holy Week**. During Holy Week, we remember important events in Jesus' life.

On Palm Sunday, we remember that Jesus rode into Jerusalem. People waved palms and called Jesus "King." Palm Sunday is also called Passion Sunday.

On Holy Thursday, we remember Jesus' Last Supper. We remember how Jesus showed his love for his friends by washing their feet.

On Good Friday, we remember that Jesus died for us.

On Holy Saturday, we remember that Jesus was buried in the tomb. We wait in hope for Easter.

Rearrange the words below. Make sentences that tell what happened during Holy Week.

yes   Jesus   to   said   God

_____

1. _____ .

saved   Jesus   us   sin   from

_____

2. _____ .

Stations of the Cross

All year we pray the Stations of the Cross.

We pray it especially during Lent and Holy Week.

Some stations tell what happened during Holy Week.

At each station, we think about Jesus. We pray.

We thank Jesus for his great love.

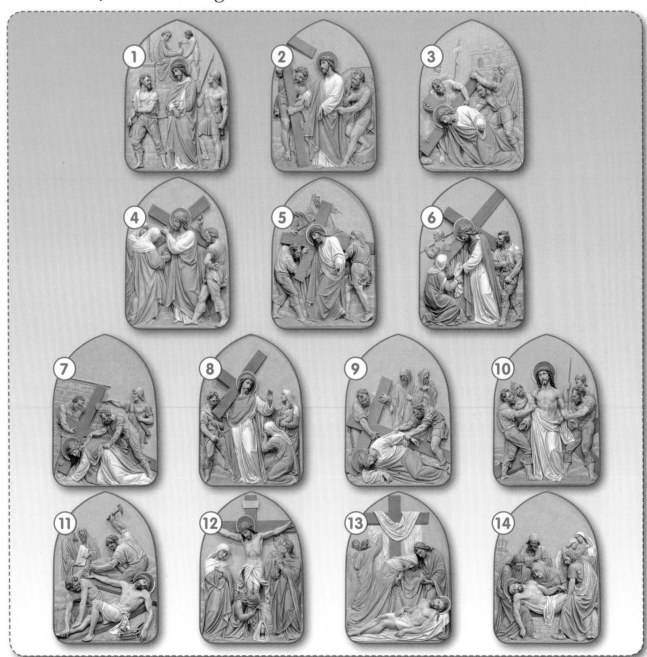

6 | Easter

Easter is the celebration of Jesus rising from the dead.

We celebrate Easter with joy.

This is the story of Easter:

> On the third day after Jesus died, Mary Magdalene went to Jesus' tomb.
> She saw that the stone was rolled away from the tomb.
> Mary Magdalene ran to tell the disciples.
> Simon Peter and another disciple ran to the tomb.
> They entered the tomb and saw that Jesus' body was not there.
>
> Then Jesus appeared to Mary Magdalene.
> She told the disciples that she had seen Jesus alive.
>
> On that same night, many of Jesus' disciples were together.
> Jesus appeared to them.
> The disciples were amazed and happy to see Jesus alive.

based on John 20:1–23

The disciples believed that Jesus is God.
They had faith.

Here is a story about Thomas.

Complete each sentence. Write the letter for the correct word.

1. Thomas did not see Jesus on _____ .

2. Thomas was not _____ .

3. He did not _____ .

4. Jesus came to see _____ .

5. He showed his hands and _____ .

6. Thomas said, "My Lord and my _____ ."

A. Easter	C. believe	E. there
B. Thomas	D. God	F. side

We have not seen Jesus as Thomas and the disciples did. We still believe that Jesus is God. We have faith.

Like Thomas, we say to Jesus, "My Lord and my God."

7 | Pentecost

Jesus promised his disciples that he would send them a helper.
He sent them the Holy Spirit.

We call the day that the Holy Spirit came Pentecost.

The Holy Spirit helped the disciples become God's new family, the Church.

This is what they did:

The disciples remembered all that Jesus had taught them.
They helped one another.
They gathered to pray and break bread together.
They did many wonderful things that showed God's love.
Everyday, more people joined them in believing that Jesus is God.

adapted from Acts 2:42–47

Draw how the disciples showed that they were God's new family, the Church.

We celebrate the gift of the Holy Spirit on Pentecost Sunday.

The Holy Spirit is given to us, too.

The Holy Spirit helps us to live as God's family, the Church.

We pray,

Come, Holy Spirit.
Fill our hearts with love.

What Catholics Should Know

(continued on next page)

(continued from page 197)

Prayer and How We Pray

Prayer is talking and listening to God. We can talk to God in the words of special prayers or in our own words. We can pray out loud or silently. We can pray to God often and in many different ways. We can praise God. We can ask him for what we need and thank him. We can pray for ourselves and for others. (See the inside front and back covers of your book for the prayers we use most often.)

Additional Catholic Prayers

It is good for us to know prayers by heart. To learn prayers by heart means that we not only learn, or memorize, the words, but try to understand and live them.

Apostles' Creed

I believe in God,
the Father almighty,
Creator of heaven and earth,
and in Jesus Christ, his only Son, our Lord,
who was conceived by the Holy Spirit,
born of the Virgin Mary,
suffered under Pontius Pilate,
was crucified, died and was buried;
he descended into hell;
on the third day he rose again from the dead;
he ascended into heaven,
and is seated at the right hand of God the Father almighty;
from there he will come to judge the living and the dead.

I believe in the Holy Spirit,
the holy catholic Church,
the communion of saints,
the forgiveness of sins,
the resurrection of the body,
and life everlasting. Amen.

Hail, Holy Queen

Hail, holy Queen, Mother of mercy,
hail, our life, our sweetness, and our hope.
To you we cry, the children of Eve;
to you we send up our sighs,
mourning and weeping in this land of exile.
Turn, then, most gracious advocate,
your eyes of mercy toward us;
lead us home at last
and show us the blessed fruit of your womb, Jesus:
O clement, O loving, O sweet Virgin Mary.

Prayer for Vocations

God, thank you for loving me.
You have called me
to live as your child.
Help all your children
to love you and one another.
Amen.

Pope Benedict XVI has suggested that certain prayers that are shared by the universal Church could be learned in Latin and prayed as a sign of the universal nature of the Church. English versions of the following prayers appear on the inside front and back covers.

Signum Crucis
(Sign of the Cross)

In nomine Patris,
et Filii,
et Spiritus Sancti.
Amen.

Gloria Patri
(Glory Be to the Father)

Gloria Patri,
et Filio,
et Spiritui Sancto.
Sicut erat in principio,
et nunc, et semper,
Et in saecula saeculorum.
Amen.

Pater Noster
(Our Father)

Pater noster, qui es in caelis,
sanctificetur nomen tuum.
Adveniat regnum tuum.
Fiat voluntas tua,
sicut in caelo et in terra.
Panem nostrum quotidianum da nobis hodie,
et dimitte nobis debita nostra
sicut et nos dimittimus debitoribus nostris.
Et ne nos inducas in tentationem,
sed libera nos a malo.
Amen.

Ave Maria
(Hail Mary)

Ave Maria, gratia plena,
Dominus tecum.
Benedicta tu in mulieribus,
et benedictus fructus ventris tui, Iesus.
Sancta Maria, Mater Dei, ora pro nobis peccatoribus,
nunc, et in hora mortis nostrae.
Amen.

The Rosary

The Rosary helps us remember the special events, or mysteries, in the lives of Jesus and Mary. We begin by praying the Sign of the Cross while holding the crucifix. Then we pray the Apostles' Creed.

We pray the Our Father as we hold the first single bead. On each of the next three beads, we pray a Hail Mary. Next, we pray a Glory Be to the Father. On the next single bead, we think about the first mystery, a particular event in the lives of Jesus and Mary. We then pray the Our Father.

Each of the 5 sets of 10 beads is called a decade. As we pray each decade, we reflect on a different mystery. Between the sets is a single bead on which we think about one of the mysteries and pray the Our Father. We then pray a Hail Mary as we hold each of the beads in the set. At the end of each set, we pray a Glory Be to the Father. In some places people pray the Hail, Holy Queen after the last decade. See page 201. We end by holding the crucifix as we pray the Sign of the Cross.

PRAYING THE ROSARY

10. Think about the fourth mystery. Pray the Our Father.

11. Pray 10 Hail Marys and a Glory Be to the Father.

9. Pray 10 Hail Marys and a Glory Be to the Father.

8. Think about the third mystery. Pray the Our Father.

6. Think about the second mystery. Pray the Our Father.

7. Pray 10 Hail Marys and a Glory Be to the Father.

5. Pray 10 Hail Marys and a Glory Be to the Father.

12. Think about the fifth mystery. Pray the Our Father.

4. Think about the first mystery. Pray the Our Father.

13. Pray 10 Hail Marys and a Glory Be to the Father.

14. Pray the Hail, Holy Queen.

3. Pray three Hail Marys and a Glory Be to the Father.

2. Pray the Our Father.

15. Pray the Sign of the Cross.

1. Pray the Sign of the Cross and the Apostles' Creed.

Stations of the Cross

The 14 Stations of the Cross represent events from Jesus' passion and death. At each station we use our senses and our imagination to remember Jesus' suffering, death, and Resurrection.

Jesus Must Die
Pontius Pilate sentences Jesus to death.

Jesus Takes His Cross
Jesus accepts his cross.

Jesus Falls
Weakened by his suffering, Jesus falls beneath the cross.

Jesus Meets His Mother
Jesus meets his Mother, Mary, who is sad to see Jesus suffer.

Simon Helps Jesus
Soldiers force Simon to carry the cross.

Veronica Helps Jesus
Veronica steps through the crowd to wipe the face of Jesus.

Jesus Falls the Second Time
Jesus falls under the weight of the cross a second time.

**The Women
Are Sorry for Jesus**
Jesus tells the women
not to cry for him.

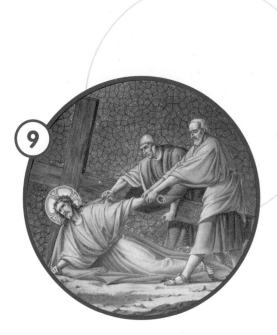

Jesus Falls Again
Jesus falls a third time.

Jesus' Clothes Are Taken Away
The soldiers take away Jesus'
clothes. They hurt him.

Jesus Is Nailed to the Cross
Jesus' hands and feet are
nailed to the cross.

Jesus Dies on the Cross
After three hours on the cross, Jesus bows his head and dies.

Jesus Is Taken Down
Mary holds Jesus in her arms.

Jesus Is Buried
Jesus' disciples place his body in the tomb.

The closing prayer— sometimes included as the 15th station—reflects on the Resurrection of Jesus.

The Seven Sacraments

The sacraments are signs of the grace we receive from God. Sacraments show that God is part of our lives. They were given to the Church by Jesus to show that he loves us. The seven sacraments help us live the way God wants us to live. The sacraments are celebrated with us by priests.

Baptism

Baptism is the first sacrament we receive. Through Baptism, we become followers of Jesus and part of God's family, the Church. The pouring of water is the main sign of Baptism. Along with Confirmation and the Eucharist, Baptism is a Sacrament of Initiation.

Confirmation

Confirmation is a Sacrament of Initiation. In this sacrament, the Holy Spirit strengthens us to be witnesses to Jesus. Confirmation makes us stronger in faith and helps us become better Christians. The bishop places holy oil in the form of a cross on our foreheads. This is the main sign of Confirmation.

The Eucharist

The Eucharist is a Sacrament of Initiation. At Mass, the bread and wine become Jesus' Body and Blood. This happens when the priest says the words of consecration that Jesus used at the Last Supper. The Eucharist is also called Holy Communion.

Penance and Reconciliation

We ask God to forgive our sins in the Sacrament of Penance and Reconciliation. The priest who celebrates this sacrament with us shares Jesus' gifts of peace and forgiveness. God always forgives us when we are sorry and do penance for our sins.

Anointing of the Sick

In this sacrament, a sick person is anointed with holy oil and receives the healing of Jesus.

Holy Orders

Some men are called to be deacons, priests, or bishops. They receive the Sacrament of Holy Orders. Through Holy Orders, the mission, or task, given by Jesus to his apostles continues in the Church.

Matrimony

Some men and women are called to be married. In the Sacrament of Matrimony, they make a solemn promise to be partners for life, both for their own good and for the good of the children they will raise.

Holy Days of Obligation

Holy Days of Obligation are the days other than Sundays on which Catholics are required to gather for Mass to celebrate the great things God has done for us through Jesus and the saints.

Six Holy Days of Obligation are celebrated in the United States.

January 1—Mary, Mother of God

40 days after Easter—Ascension (in many U.S. dioceses, the Seventh Sunday of Easter)

August 15— Assumption of the Blessed Virgin Mary

November 1—All Saints

December 8—Immaculate Conception

December 25—Nativity of Our Lord Jesus Christ

Commandments

The Ten Commandments

God gave us the Ten Commandments. They teach us how to live for God and for others. They help us follow the moral law to do good and avoid evil.

1. I am your God; love no one or anything more than me.
2. Use God's name with respect.
3. Keep the Lord's day holy.
4. Honor and obey your parents.
5. Treat all human life with respect.
6. Respect your body and the bodies of others.
7. Respect what belongs to others.
8. Tell the truth.
9. In marriage, husbands and wives respect each other.
10. Be happy with what you have.

The Great Commandment

People asked Jesus, "What is the most important commandment?" Jesus said, "First, love God. Love him with your heart, soul, and mind. The second is like it: Love your neighbor as much as you love yourself." (adapted from Matthew 22:37–39) We call this the Great Commandment.

The New Commandment

Before his death on the cross, Jesus gave his disciples a new commandment: "Love one another. As I have loved you, so you also should love one another." (adapted from John 13:34)

Making Good Choices

The Holy Spirit helps us make good choices. We get help from the Ten Commandments, the grace of the sacraments, and the teachings of the Church. We also get help from the example of the saints and fellow Christians. To make good choices, we should ask ourselves the following questions:

1. Is the thing I am choosing to do a good thing?
2. Am I choosing to do it for the right reasons?
3. Am I choosing to do it at the right time and in the right place?

The Bible

God speaks to us in many ways. One way is through the Bible. The Bible is the story of God's promise to care for us, especially through his Son, Jesus. The Bible is made up of two parts. The Old Testament tells stories about God and the Jewish people before Jesus was born. In the New Testament, Jesus teaches us about the Father's love. The Gospels tell stories about Jesus' life, death, and Resurrection. At Mass, we hear stories from the Bible. We can also read the Bible on our own.

Showing Our Love for the World

Jesus taught us to care for those in need. The social teachings of the Church call us to follow Jesus' example in each of the following areas:

Life and Dignity

God wants us to care for everyone. We are all made in God's image.

Family and Community

Jesus wants us to be loving helpers in our families and communities.

Rights and Responsibilities
All people should have what they need to live good lives.

The Poor and Vulnerable
Jesus calls us to do what we can to help people in need.

Work and Workers
The work that we do gives glory to God.

Solidarity

Since God is our Father, we are called to treat everyone in the world as brothers and sisters.

God's Creation

We show our love for God's world by taking care of it.

Glossary

A

absolution the forgiveness of God. In the Sacrament of Penance and Reconciliation, we say that we are sorry for our sins. Then the priest offers us God's absolution.

altar the table in the church on which the priest celebrates Mass.

ambo a platform from which a person reads the Word of God during Mass

angel a messenger from God

apostle one of twelve special men who followed Jesus and saw him after the Resurrection. These were the people sent to preach the Gospel to the whole world.

B

Baptism the first of the three sacraments by which we become members of the Church. Baptism frees us from original sin and gives us new life in Jesus Christ through the Holy Spirit.

Baptism

Bible the written story of God's promise to care for us, especially through his Son, Jesus

bishop a leader in the Church. Bishops teach us what God is asking of us as followers of Jesus today.

Blessed Sacrament the Body of Christ. It is kept in the tabernacle to be adored and to be taken to the sick and the dying.

Body and Blood of Christ the bread and wine consecrated by the priest at Mass

C

catholic a word that means "all over the world." The Church is catholic because Jesus gave the Church to the whole world.

Christ a title, like *Messiah*, that means "anointed with oil." This name is given to Jesus after the Resurrection.

Christian the name given to people who want to live as Jesus taught us to live

Christmas the day on which we celebrate the birth of Jesus

Church the name given to the followers of Christ all over the world. Spelled with a small *c*, the church is the building where we gather to pray to God.

commandment a rule that tells us how to live as God wants us to live

confession the act of telling our sins to a priest in the Sacrament of Penance and Reconciliation

Confirmation the sacrament that completes the grace we receive in Baptism

contrition the sadness we feel when we know that we have sinned

creation everything that God has made. God said that all creation is good.

Creator God, who made everything that is

Christmas

Easter

D

deacon a man who accepts God's call to serve the Church. Deacons help the bishop and priests in the work of the Church.

disciple a person who is a follower of Jesus and tries to live as he did

E

Easter the celebration of the raising of Jesus Christ from the dead. Easter is the most important Christian feast.

Emmanuel a name that means "God with us." It is a name given to Jesus.

disciple

Eucharist the sacrament in which we give thanks to God for giving us Jesus Christ. We receive the Body and Blood of Jesus Christ in Holy Communion.

The Gospel is read at Mass.

F

faith a gift of God. Faith helps us believe in God and live as he wants us to live.

G

Gospel the good news of God's love for us. We learn this news in the story of Jesus' life, death, and Resurrection. The story is presented to us in the Gospels of Matthew, Mark, Luke, and John.

grace the gift of God given to us without our earning it. Sanctifying grace fills us with God's life and makes us his friends.

Great Commandment Jesus' important teaching that we are to love both God and other people

H

heaven the life with God that is full of happiness and never ends

holy describing the kind of life we live when we cooperate with the grace of God

Holy Communion the Body and Blood of Jesus Christ that we receive at Mass

Holy Family the family made up of Jesus; his mother, Mary; and his foster father, Joseph

Holy Spirit the third Person of the Trinity, who comes to us in Baptism and fills us with God's life

J

Jesus the Son of God, who was born of the Virgin Mary, died, was raised from the dead, and saves us so that we can live with God forever

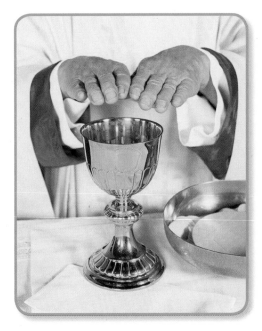

Holy Communion

Joseph the foster father of Jesus, who was engaged to Mary when the angel announced that Mary would have a child through the power of the Holy Spirit

L

Last Supper the last meal Jesus ate with his disciples on the night before he died. Every Mass is a remembrance of that last meal.

Lord's Day Sunday, the day on which Jesus rose from the dead. It is a special day for Christians to worship God.

Joseph and Jesus

parish

M

Mary the mother of Jesus. She is called "full of grace" because God chose her to be Jesus' mother.

Mass our most important means of praying to God. At Mass we listen to God's Word, the Bible. We receive the Body and Blood of Jesus Christ in the form of bread and wine in Holy Communion.

miracle acts of wonder that cannot be explained by natural causes. They are works of God. In the Gospels, Jesus works miracles as a sign that God is present in his ministry.

N

New Testament the story of Jesus and the early Church

O

Old Testament the story of God's plan for the salvation of all people

original sin the result of the sin of Adam and Eve. They disobeyed God and chose to follow their own will rather than God's will.

P

parish a community of believers in Jesus Christ who meet regularly to worship God together

Passover the Jewish festival that commemorates the delivery of God's people from slavery in Egypt. In the Eucharist we celebrate our passover from death to life through Jesus' death and Resurrection.

penance the turning away from sin because we want to live as God wants us to live (*See* Sacrament of Penance and Reconciliation.)

pope the bishop of Rome, successor of Saint Peter, and leader of the Roman Catholic Church

prayer the raising of our hearts and minds to God. We are able to speak to and listen to God in prayer because he teaches us how to do so.

priest a man who accepts God's special call to serve the Church. Priests guide the Church and lead it in the celebration of the sacraments.

R

reconciliation making friends again after a friendship has been broken by some action or lack of action. In the Sacrament of Penance and Reconciliation, we are reconciled with God, the Church, and others.

Resurrection the bodily raising of Jesus Christ from the dead on the third day after he died on the cross

S

sacrament the way in which God enters our life. Through simple objects such as water, oil, and bread, Jesus continues to bless us.

Sacrament of Penance and Reconciliation the sacrament in which we celebrate God's forgiveness of our sins when we say to the priest that we are sorry for them

sacrifice a gift given to God to give him thanks. Jesus' death on the cross was the greatest sacrifice.

saint a holy person who died as a true friend of God and now lives with God forever

Savior Jesus, the Son of God, who became human to make us friends with God again. The name *Jesus* means "God saves."

Savior

sin a choice to do what is wrong on purpose. A sin is when you say no to God.

T

tabernacle the container in which the Blessed Sacrament is kept so that Holy Communion can be taken to the sick and the dying

temptation a thought or feeling that can lead us to disobey God. Temptation can come either from outside us or inside us.

Ten Commandments the 10 rules that God gave to Moses. The Ten Commandments sum up God's law and show us how to live as his children.

Trinity the mystery of one God, existing in three Persons: the Father, the Son, and the Holy Spirit

Index

quiet of, 36–39
thanking (*see* thanking God and Jesus)
trusting, 19, 22
water, gift of, 29
world, made the, 10 (*see also* Creation)
Good Friday, 136, 138, 191
Good News, 170. *See also* Gospel
Good Shepherd, 115, 116, 118
activity page, 119
lost sheep, 116, 126, 127
Gospel, 165, 224
grace, 62, 224
Great Commandment, 215, 224

H

Hail Mary, 69, 164, 203
Hail, Holy Queen, 201
"Happy Birthday, Dear Jesus" (song), 187
heaven, 62, 224
holy, 224
Holy Communion, 134, 211, 225. *See also*
       Eucharist; Last Supper; Mass
Holy Days of Obligation, 214
Holy Family, 80, 225
Holy Father, 155. *see also* pope
Holy Orders, 213
Holy Saturday, 191
Holy Spirit, 147, 152, 216, 225. *See also* God
apostles, received by, 148, 149
Baptism, presence at, 150
Christians, helping the first, 166
gifts from, 180c
glory to God, 172
guidance for us, 180c
Jesus, helping us know, 165
light of, 167
Pentecost, 195, 196
tongues of fire, 148
Holy Thursday, 133, 138, 144, 191
Holy Week, 132, 191
hope, 151
Hosanna, 131
How the Grinch Stole Christmas, 88d
hurting others, 122

I

Immaculate Conception, 214
Immaculate Mary, 161. *See also* Mary
Initiation, Sacrament of, 210. *See also*
       Baptism, Eucharist, Reconciliation

J

Jairus, 99
James, Saint, 92
Jesus, 225. *See also* Good Shepherd
birth, 74 (*see also* Christmas)
brings dead girl back to life, 99
care for us, 94
children, love for, 4, 8
cures a sick man, 98
death on the cross, 8
following his example, 218–19
friend, 4, 97
Good Shepherd (*see* Good Shepherd)
healing, 98, 99
light of the world, 32
love for all, 5, 149
miracles, 98, 99
path to, activity, 55
presence in our lives, 180a, 180b
Son of God, 67
storm, calming, 94
talking to him in our heart, 6
thanking (*see* thanking God and Jesus)
with us always, 175
"Jesus Loves Me" (song), 88
John, Saint, 92, 106, 165, 184
Joseph, Saint, 70, 88c, 184, 225
Julie Billiart, Saint, 32, 184

K

kneeling, when we pray, 25
knowledge, 180c

L

lambs, 116
Last Supper, 133, 134, 144, 211, 225
Latin, prayers in, 202, 203
lay ministers, 95

Lent, 189
light of Holy Spirit, 167. *See also* Holy Spirit
Little Drummer Boy, The, 88d
liturgical calendar, 182
Lord's Day, 225
Lord's Prayer. *See* Our Father
love, 150. *See also* loving heart
    God's, for us, 97, 102, 128a
    God, our love for him, 103, 104, 107,
        108, 125
    others as ourselves, 5, 109, 110, 111, 112,
        113, 114, 125, 128a
    parents as nurturers of, 128a
    spreading Jesus', 169, 170
    virtue of, 151
loving heart, 128c, 128d. *See also* love
Luke, Saint, 165

M

Magi, 88d. *See also* Wise Men
manger, 74, 88c
Mark, Saint, 165
Martin, Saint, 168
Mary, 226
    activity, 163, 164
    Annunciation, 67
    blessed, 68
    chosen by God, 67
    Holy Spirit, receives, 148
    Jesus' birth, 88c
    Mother of God, 69, 159, 164, 214
    Queen of Heaven, 160, 164
    role model, 162
    visit to Elizabeth, 68
Mary (mother of James and Salome), 129
Mary Magdalene, 129, 193
Mass, 82, 118, 144, 226
    Bible stories during, 217
    celebration of Jesus' gifts, 134, 138
    drawing activity, 84, 135
    family meal, 138
Matrimony, Sacrament of, 213
Matthew, Saint, 165
Messiah, 88c, 222. *See also* Jesus
miracle, 226

missionaries
    helpers of Jesus, 95
Morning Offering, 105
Moses
    friend of God, 23
    listener of God, 23
    Prayer of, 24
    worshipper of God, 24

N

Nativity of Our Lord Jesus Christ, 214
Nativity scene, 88b, 88d
neighbors, loving, 109, 110, 111
New Commandment, 215
New Testament, 217, 226
Nicholas, Saint, 88b

O

obeying God, 121
    lost lambs, 116, 126
    sorry, saying, when we do not, 123
"O Come, All Ye Faithful" (song), 187
oil, holy, 212
Old Testament, 217, 226
original sin, 226
Our Father, 22, 23, 53, 203
    Jesus taught us, 51, 54
    prayer, 52

P

Palm Sunday, 131, 132, 138, 191
parents, love and caring for us, 20
parish, 226
    caring for others, 83
    Church family, 81
    worship together, 82
Passover, 226
Pater Noster, 203. *See also* Our Father
patron saints, 184
peace, 143, 144, 152
Peace Prayer, 145
peace, sign of, 118
penance, 212, 226

Penance and Reconciliation, Sacrament of, 227

Pentecost, 195, 196

Peter, Saint, 92, 154

piety, 180c

poor, caring for, 219

pope, 154, 155, 158, 226

Posadas, Las, 88b

praising God, responsive reading, 58

prayer, 227. *See also* prayers, specific
    bedtime, 96
    drawing activity, 49
    how Catholics pray, 199
    Jesus' teaching, 51, 52, 53, 54
    listening to God during, 44
    loving heart, 128c
    mealtime, 48, 50
    morning, 48
    Morning Offering, 105
    Moses, of, 24
    night, 48
    Our Father (*see* Our Father)
    Peace Prayer, 145
    types of, 50
    visiting with God, 45

Prayer of Moses, 24

prayers, specific. *See also* prayer
    Apostles' Creed, 200
    Ave Maria, 203
    Glory Be to the Father, 172, 176, 202
    Hail Mary (*see* Hail Mary)
    Hail, Holy Queen, 201
    Pater Noster, 203
    Rosary (*see* Rosary)
    Sign of the Cross (*see* Sign of the Cross)
    Stations of the Cross (*see* Stations of the Cross)
    Vocations, for, 201

priest, 95, 213, 227
    Baptism, role during, 156
    helper of Jesus, 95
    Holy Communion, role in, 134, 135

promises of God, 64, 66

Psalm 23, "The Lord is my shepherd," prayer, 117, 120

R

reconciliation, 212, 227. *See also* Penance and Reconciliation, Sacrament of

Resurrection, 140, 146, 222, 227. *See also* Easter

Rosary, 204, 205

Rudolph the Red-Nosed Reindeer, 88d

S

sacraments, 210–13, 227

sacrifice, 227

saints, 183, 227. *See also specific names*
    patron (*see* patron saints)

Samuel, 43, 45

Savior, 63, 64, 138, 142, 227. *See also* Jesus

seed story, 12–14

selfishness, 123

sharing with others, 19

shepherds, 75, 88c

sign of peace, 118

Sign of the Cross, 6, 7, 8, 25, 152, 202
    Ash Wednesday, on, 189
    Baptism, made during, 58b, 58d

Signum Crucis, 202. *See also* Sign of the Cross

Simon Peter, 193

sin, 228. *See also* obeying God
    forgiving, 128
    hurting others, 122

sisters, religious
    helpers of Jesus, 95

solidarity, 220

sorry, telling God we are, 47, 119, 123, 128

Spirit, 58a. *See also* Holy Spirit

stable, 74

Stations of the Cross, 192, 206–9

T

tabernacle, 228

temptation, 228

Ten Commandments, 215, 228

Teresa of Calcutta, Blessed, 128c

thanking God and Jesus, 11, 47

Creation, for the wonder of, 16
love, for his, 19
responsive litany, 87
responsive song, 57
Thérèse, Saint, 163
Thomas, Saint, 194
Trinity, 228
trust in God, 19

U

understanding, 180c

V

Very Important Persons (activity), 21
virtues, 150, 151
Vocations, Prayer for, 201
vulnerable, caring for, 219

W

"We Love Our Good Father" (song), 57
wine, 133
wisdom, 180c
Wise Men, 76. *See also* Magi
world, caring for, 11, 218, 220
wreath, Advent, 186. *See also* Advent

Scripture Index

OLD TESTAMENT

Genesis
1:1, pp. 10, 31, 57

Exodus
33:13, pp.18, 24

1 Samuel
3:9, pp. 42, 44

1 Chronicles
16:34, p. 16

Psalms
5:8, p. 28
9:2, p. 47
10:17, p. 102
17:6, p. 50
18:2, p. 108
23, p. 117
23:1, p. 120
23:1–3, p. 120
33:22, p. 34
34:9, p. 46
38:19, p. 47
40:14, pp. 46, 66

52:10, p. 22
72:19, p. 96
118:1, p. 138
119:111, p. 42
133:1, p. 85
145:8–10, p. 89
146:9, p. 114

NEW TESTAMENT

Matthew
2:10–11, p. 88a
5:14, p. 167
5:16, p. 170
6:25–34, p. 19
6:31–33, p. 22
6:6, p. 50
7:24, p. 42
22:36–37, p. 108
22:37–39, pp. 128a, 215
25:34–36, p. 102
28:19–20, p.158

Mark
10:14, p. 8
12:28–30, pp. 103, 107
12:43–44, p. 114

16:6–7, p. 129

Luke
1:38, p. 72
2:1–7, p.187
2:1–18, p. 88c
2:8–16, p. 188
2:14, pp. 78, 88b
10:2, p. 96
18:16, p. 4
22:19–20, p. 138
24:30–31, p. 146

John
3:16, p. 59, 87
8:12, p. 32
10:11, pp. 116, 120
13:34, p. 215
15:5, p. 180a
19:26–27, p. 164
20:1–23, p. 193
20:21–22, p. 152
21:17, p. 154

Acts of the Apostles
2:42–47, p. 195

Romans
6:3-5, p. 58d
8:14, p. 1

1 Corinthians
10:31, p. 179

Galatians
3:36–38, p. 58d

Ephesians
4:1–6, p. 58d

1 John
3:5, p. 66
4:9, p. 34

Art Credits

When there is more than one picture on a page, credits are supplied in sequence, left to right, top to bottom. Page positions are abbreviated as follows: (t) top, (c) center, (b) bottom, (l) left, (r) right.

FRONT MATTER:
iii(t) © The Crosiers/Gene Plaisted OSC

UNIT 1:
3(b) © The Crosiers/Gene Plaisted OSC
4 Sally Schaedler
7 Phil Martin Photography
9(b) Nan Brooks
11(l) © Photo Network/Alamy
12(tr) Nan Brooks
12(bl) Nan Brooks
13 Nan Brooks
14 Nan Brooks
17(b) Robert Voigts
19(tr) © The Crosiers/Gene Plaisted OSC
22 Len Ebert/PC&F Inc.
23(b) Tim Sperling
24(t) © The Crosiers/Gene Plaisted OSC
25 Nan Brooks
26(tl) W. P. Wittman Limited
26(tr) Phil Martin Photography
26(c) James L. Shaffer
26(br) Myrleen Ferguson Cate/PhotoEdit, Inc.
28 © The Crosiers/Gene Plaisted OSC
29(t) Phil Martin Photography
30(t,b) Phil Martin Photography
31(b) Kelly Neil
35(t) Getty/Yellow Dog Productions
36-37 Ginna Hirtenstein
38-39 Tom Sperling
40(b) Cleo Freelance Photography
41(t) Kelly Neil
43(b) © The Crosiers/Gene Plaisted OSC
45 © The Crosiers/Gene Plaisted OSC
48(t) © EyeWire
51(b) Sally Schaedler
53(t) © The Crosiers/Gene Plaisted OSC
53(b) W. P. Wittman Limited
54 Ginna Hirtenstein
55(b) Len Ebert/PC&FC Inc.
57-58 © The Crosiers/Gene Plaisted OSC
58a Phil Martin Photography
58b © The Crosiers/Gene Plaisted OSC
58c(tr) Phil Martin Photography
58c(br) Phil Martin Photography

UNIT 2:
59-60 © The Crosiers/Gene Plaisted OSC
62-63 Len Ebert/PC&F Inc.
64 Tom Sperling
67(bl) © The Crosiers/Gene Plaisted OSC
68-69 Polly Lewis
70(t) Anonymous Brazil
72(tr) Len Ebert/PC&F Inc.
72(b) © The Crosiers/Gene Plaisted OSC

73(t) Getty/Yellow Dog Productions
73(b) © The Crosiers/Gene Plaisted OSC
74-76 Polly Lewis
77(b) Nan Brooks
78 Polly Lewis
79(t) © The Crosiers/Gene Plaisted OSC
80 Polly Lewis
81(t) © Myrleen Cate/PhotoEdit, Inc.
81(c) IHM Mission
81(c) © James Shaffer/PhotoEdit, Inc.
82 © Craig Lovell/Corbis
83 © Myrleen Cate/PhotoEdit, Inc.
86(tl) Polly Lewis
86(tr) Len Ebert/PC&F Inc.
86(cl,cr,bl,br) Polly Lewis
87-88 © The Crosiers/Gene Plaisted OSC
88b(b) © A. Ramey/PhotoEdit, Inc.
88c © The Crosiers/Gene Plaisted OSC
88d(b) © John Springer Collection/Corbis

Unit 3:
91(b) Sally Schaedler
92 Emily Friel
93(cr) © Danny Lehman/Corbis
94 Sally Schaedler
95(t) © John Springer Collection/Corbis
97(b) © The Crosiers/Gene Plaisted OSC
98(b) Len Ebert/PC&F Inc.
99 © The Crosiers/Gene Plaisted OSC
100 Sally Schaedler
101 Nan Brooks
103(b) Nan Brooks
106 © The Crosiers/Gene Plaisted OSC
109(b) Tom Sperling
110 Nan Brooks
112 Sally Schaedler
115(b) © The Crosiers/Gene Plaisted OSC
116 Sally Schaedler
117 Tom Sperling
118 Phil Martin Photography
120(t) Ginna Hirtenstein
120(b) Tom Sperling
121(b) © The Crosiers/Gene Plaisted OSC
123 © Myrleen Ferguson Cate/Photoedit
124(t) Emily Friel
124(b) Ginna Hirtenstein
125 Len Ebert/PC&F Inc.
127(t) © The Crosiers/Gene Plaisted OSC
128 © The Crosiers/Gene Plaisted OSC

UNIT 4:
129-130 © The Crosiers/Gene Plaisted OSC
131(t) © Reuters/Corbis
131(b) © The Crosiers/Gene Plaisted OSC
132(tl) © Jose Pedro Fernandes/Alamy
133 Sally Schaedler
134(bl) Phil Martin Photography
134(br) © The Crosiers/Gene Plaisted OSC
136-137 Sally Schaedler

138 Melissa Kupfer
139(b) Ginna Hirtenstein
140-141 Sally Schaedler
142(b) Len Ebert/PC&F Inc.
143 Len Ebert/PC&F Inc.
145 © The Crosiers/Gene Plaisted OSC
146(t) W. P. Wittman Limited
147(t) Tim Graham/Getty Images
147(b) Sally Schaedler
148(b) Polly Lewis
149(b) © The Crosiers/Gene Plaisted OSC
152 Melissa Kupfer
153-154 © The Crosiers/Gene Plaisted OSC
155 AFP/Getty Images
159-160 © The Crosiers/Gene Plaisted OSC
161(t) Polly Lewis
163(t) © Office Central de Lisieux
164 Melissa Kupfer
165(b) Tom Sperling
168 © The Crosiers/Gene Plaisted OSC
172 © Reg Charity/Corbis
178 Sally Schaedler
179-180 © The Crosiers/Gene Plaisted OSC
180c © The Crosiers/Gene Plaisted OSC

SPECIAL SEASONS AND LESSONS:
181 © The Crosiers/Gene Plaisted OSC
182 Susan Tolonen
183 © Carmen Sedano/ Alamy
184 © The Crosiers/Gene Plaisted OSC
190 Robert Voigts
192 © The Crosiers/Gene Plaisted OSC
193(t) © The Crosiers/Gene Plaisted OSC
194 Sally Schaedler

WHAT CATHOLICS SHOULD KNOW:
202 © Vatican Pool/Corbis
203(t) © The Crosiers/Gene Plaisted OSC
205 Greg Kuepfer
206–209 © The Crosiers/Gene Plaisted OSC
210 Phil Martin Photography
211(t) Phil Martin Photography
211(c) © Myrleen Ferguson Cate/PhotoEdit
212(t) © Myrleen Ferguson Cate/PhotoEdit
212(b) © Alan Oddie/PhotoEdit
214 © Tony Freeman/PhotoEdit

GLOSSARY:
224(t) Phil Martin Photography
227 © The Crosiers/Gene Plaisted OSC

LESSON PULLOUTS:
235(t) Nan Brooks
235(cl) Dick Mlodock
235(cr) Robert Korta
235(b) Cheryl Arnemann
236 Phyllis Pollema-Cahill
The Way of the Cross: Nan Brooks
Scripture Prayer Booklet, 1,12: Dick Mlodock
Scripture Prayer Booklet, 2: Tim Basaldua

Scripture Prayer Booklet, 5: Yoshi Miyake
Scripture Prayer Booklet, 6-7: Robert Korta
Scripture Prayer Booklet, 8: Dick Mlodock
Scripture Prayer Booklet, 12: Dick Mlodock
Punchouts 1: Nan Brooks
Punchouts 2(t): Cheryl Arnemann
Punchouts 2(b): Len Ebert
Punchouts 4: Len Ebert
Punchouts 5(tl): Monica Paxson
Punchouts 5(tr): Len Ebert
Punchouts 6(tl): Monica Paxson
Punchouts 6(tr): Len Ebert
Punchouts 7: Len Ebert
Punchouts 8: Rober Korta

Lesson Pullouts

- **The Way of the Cross**

- **Scripture prayer booklet**

"I am with you always, until the end of time."

adapted from Matthew 28:20

Jesus, you rose from the dead on Easter Sunday.

† You gave God's life to us.

  Thank you, Jesus!

†

Way of the Cross

Jesus, I want to follow you as I pray the Stations of the Cross.

This booklet belongs to

---

13 Jesus Is Taken Down

Mary held Jesus in her arms.

† Mary, help me to love Jesus as you love him.

†

2 Jesus Takes His Cross

Jesus took the heavy cross with love.

† Jesus, help me to do hard things with love.

†

1 Jesus Must Die

Some of the people wanted Jesus to die.

† Jesus, you were willing to die for us.

Thank you, Jesus.

14 Jesus Is Buried

The friends of Jesus put him in the tomb.

† Jesus, you died to save us.

You rose to bring us new life.

3 Jesus Falls

The heavy cross made Jesus fall.

† Jesus, it was hard to carry the cross.

You carried it to save us from sin.

1 Jesus Must Die

12 Jesus Dies on the Cross

After three hours, Jesus died on the cross.

† Jesus, you died so we can live with God in heaven.

Thank you for loving us so much.

11 Jesus Is Nailed to the Cross

Jesus forgave the people who hurt him.

He prayed,
    "Father, forgive them."

† Jesus, teach me to forgive others who hurt me.

4 Jesus Meets His Mother

Mary was sad to see Jesus suffer.

She knew he must die for her and for us.

† Thank you, Mary, for being the Mother of our Savior.

9 Jesus Falls Again

Jesus fell again under his cross.

He was very tired, but he did not stop.

† Jesus, help me to always try to be good.

6 Veronica Helps Jesus

Veronica was sorry for Jesus.

She wiped his face.

† Jesus, help me to be kind as Veronica was.

5 Simon Helps Jesus

Jesus found it hard to carry
the heavy cross by himself.

Simon helped him.

† Jesus, show me how to
help others.

10 Jesus' Clothes Are Taken Away

The soldiers took away
Jesus' clothes.

They hurt him.

† Jesus, you suffered for us.

Thank you.

7 Jesus Falls the Second Time

Jesus fell a second time.

He got up and carried
the cross again.

† Thank you, Jesus, for
carrying your cross for us.

8 The Women Are Sorry for Jesus

Some women cried to see
Jesus suffer.

He spoke to them.

† Jesus, teach me to care when
others suffer and to help them.

Daniel Trusts God

Trust in the LORD and do good.

Psalm 37:3

Daniel was a good man. He loved God and prayed to him every day. Daniel was also a good leader in his country. But the other leaders were jealous of Daniel. They wanted to get him in trouble. So they said to the king,

"Make a law that no one may pray for 30 days. Anyone who prays will be thrown to the lions." The king made the law. Because Daniel loved God, he kept praying to him three times a day. The king liked Daniel, but it was too late to change his law. Daniel was thrown into a den of lions.

The next morning the king went to the den of lions. Daniel was there. He was unhurt because he trusted in God.

adapted from Daniel 6:2–29

12

Scripture prayer booklet

I Love Jesus.

Jesus Loves Me.

Name _____

We Pray to God Using Psalm Prayers

You are great, and you do wondrous deeds.
You are my God.
Teach me, O LORD, your way.

adapted from Psalm 86:10–11

LORD, you know me.
You know everything I do.
You know how I think.
You are always with me.
You are everywhere!

adapted from Psalm 139:1–5

I am sad.
Have you forgotten me, God?
Why are you so sad, my soul?
Hope in God.
I shall again thank God!

adapted from Psalm 42:10,12

Prayer Chain
Color a prayer bead every time you use this booklet.

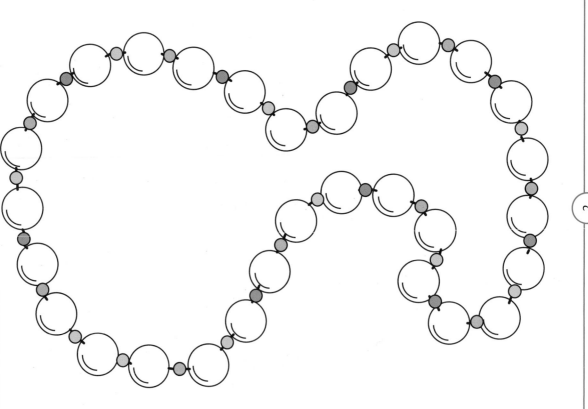

Jesus Gives the Gift of Himself

Jesus took the bread and blessed it. He broke the bread and said, "Take this and eat it. This is my body."

Then Jesus took the chalice of wine. He gave thanks and said, "Drink from this chalice. This is my blood."

adapted from Matthew 26:26–28

Whenever you eat this bread and drink this chalice, you proclaim the death of Jesus until he comes in glory.

adapted from 1 Corinthians 11:26

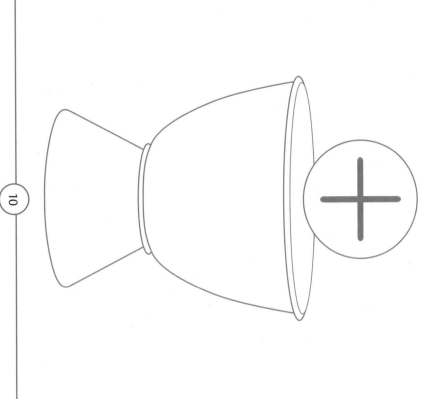

Jesus Shows His Great Love for Us

God showed his great love for us. Christ died for us.

adapted from Romans 5:8

God is rich in mercy and loves us very much. He brought us to life with Christ and raised us up with him.

adapted from Ephesians 2:4–6

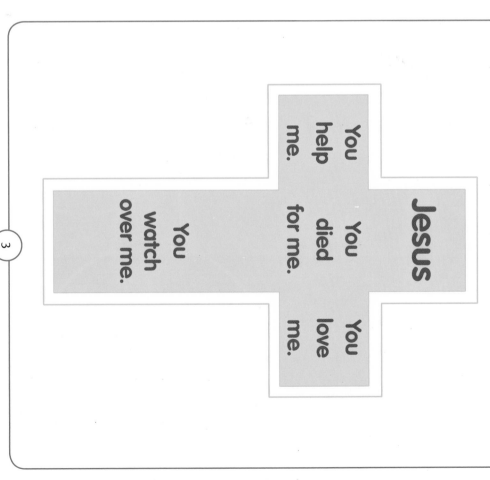

Jesus

You died for me.

You help me.

You love me.

You watch over me.

We Tell God We Are Sorry

Write in the heart what you are sorry for.

I am sorry for . . .

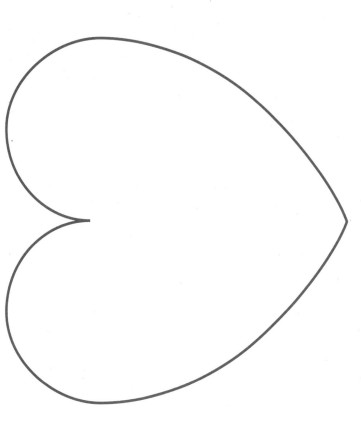

Have mercy on me, God. Cleanse me from my sin.
Create a clean heart in me.

adapted from Psalm 51:2,4,12

**Talk to Jesus in the quiet of your heart.
Ask him for his forgiveness. Listen to Jesus.
Thank him for his love and forgiveness.**

God Loves All of Creation

God saw all that he had made.
It was very good.

adapted from Genesis 1:31

Draw some of your favorite things.

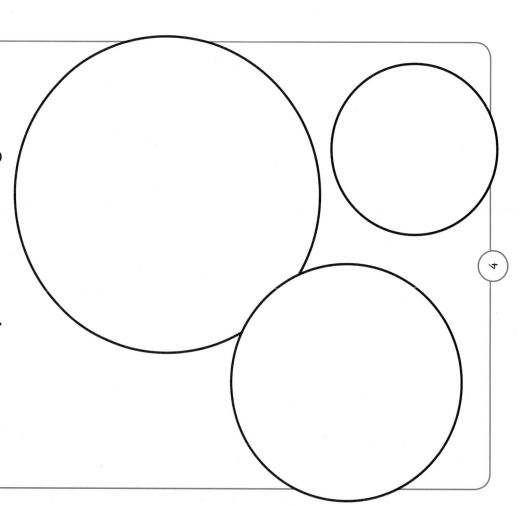

God Looks for Us

Jesus told this story.

A woman had 10 coins.
She lost one. She searched
for it.

She lit a lamp and swept
the floor.

When she found the coin, she called her friends
together. She said, "Rejoice with me. I found my
lost coin."

adapted from Luke 15:8–10

When we go away from God,
God searches for us and calls us back to him.

Jesus Helps Us Be Like Him

Jesus teaches people that God
loves them.

See John 10:1–18.

Jesus helps the sick.

See Luke 18:35–43.

Jesus gives food
to the hungry.

See Mark 6:34–44.

Mary Shows Us How to Love God and Others

Mary visited her relative Elizabeth.

See Luke 2:39–56.

Mary cared for Jesus and taught him many things.

See Luke 2:40.

Mary listened to God's angel. She said yes to God.

See Luke 2:26–38.

Mary praised God for choosing her to be the mother of Jesus.

See Luke 1:46–55.

Punchouts

Christian

I will help.

I will help.

I will help.

I will help.

VIP

You are a
very important
person.

VIP

You are a
very important
person.

VIP

You are a
very important
person.

VIP

You are a
very important
person.

Chapter 11

Chapter 11

Chapter 11

Chapter 11

Chapter 3

Chapter 3

Chapter 3

Chapter 3

Special Seasons & Lessons, 8 ↓

To the Guardian Angel
Angel sent by God
    to guide me,

be my light and
    walk beside me;

be my guardian
    and protect me;

in the paths of life
    direct me.

Amen.

Morning Offering
O Jesus, I offer you
all I think, do, and say.

Bless me and make me
like you today.
Amen.

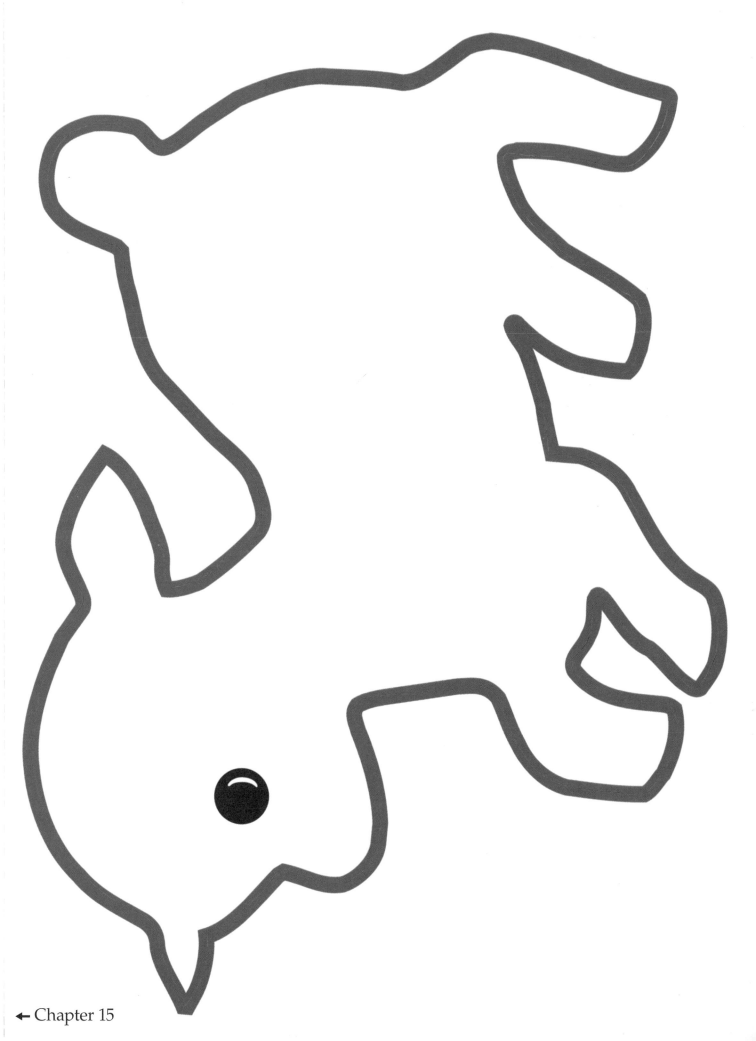

Chapter 18

© LOYOLAPRESS.

Chapter 10

Chapter 11

Fold front

Fold back

Fold front

Join strips at the end notches
to form rings for the bases.

Insert figures in
the side notches
to stand.

©LOYOLAPRESS.

©LOYOLAPRESS.

©LOYOLAPRESS.

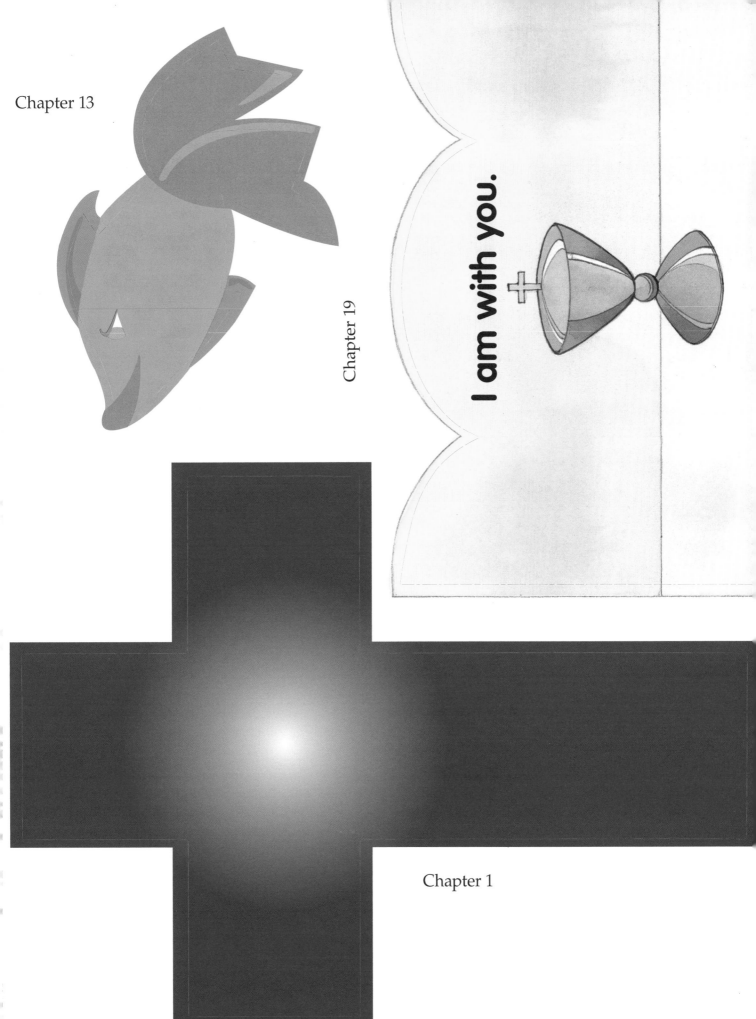

Chapter 13

Chapter 19

I am with you.

Chapter 1

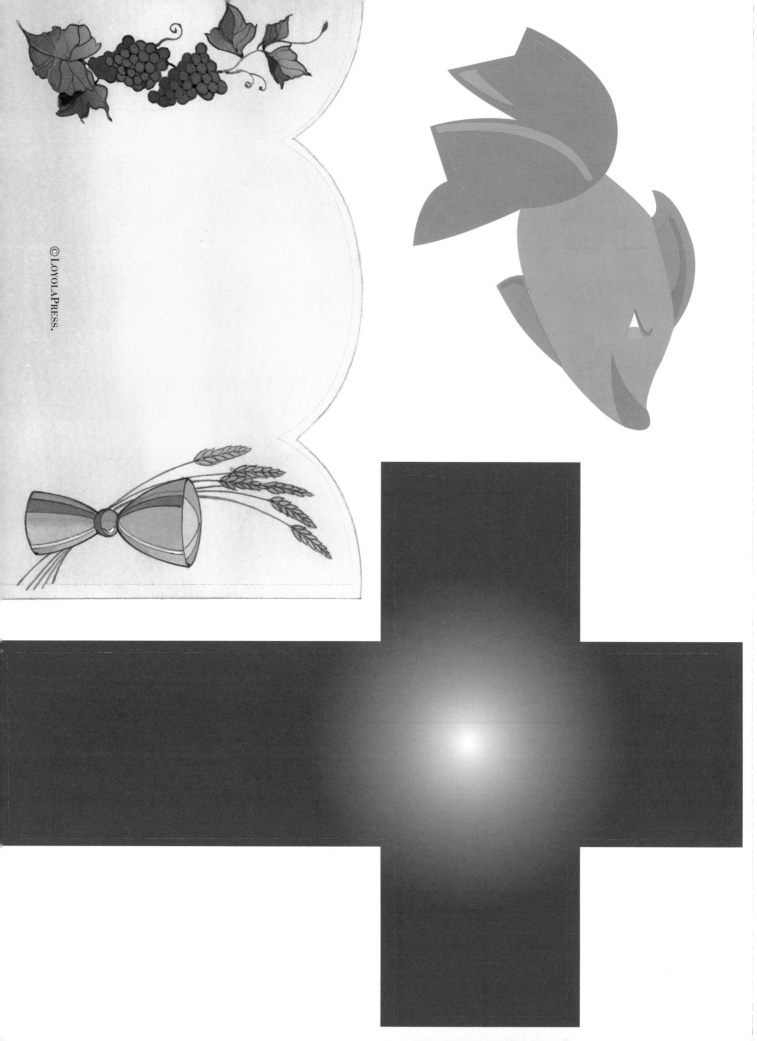

© LOYOLAPRESS.

Fold

**Bless us, O Lord,
and these your gifts.**

Fold

Lord, every morning I pray to you,
and at night I come before you.

adapted from Psalm 5:3; 77:3

Chapter 7

Chapter 7

©LOYOLAPRESS.

JOY

God
is my
Father.

Christian

Glory
to
God

Mary Mary Mary

Jesus
Chapter 1

Chapter 9

Chapter 3

Chapter 20

Chapter 5

Chapter 10

Chapter 23

Chapter 25